Authentic Mexican Cooking

by Paula Holt
and Hélène Juarez

A Fireside Book
Published by Simon & Schuster, Inc.
New York

A Fireside Book published by Simon & Schuster, Inc.

Simon & Schuster Building, Rockefeller Center,
1230 Avenue of the Americas, New York,
New York 10020

FIRESIDE and colophon are registered trademarks
of Simon & Schuster, Inc.

Designed by Barbara M. Marks

Manufactured in the United States of America

10 9 8 7 6

Library of Congress Cataloging in Publication Data

Holt, Paula.
  Authentic Mexican cooking.

  "A Fireside book."
  Includes index.
  1. Cookery, Mexican.   I. Juarez, Hélène.
  II. Title.
TX716.M4H65   1984   641.5972   84-10652
ISBN: 0-671-50496-7

Contents

Foreword

There is a special quality about Mexican food . . . it is by its very nature a bit more festive, more adventurous, and more fun than its North American counterparts. Even the lowliest taco from a franchised taco stand offers a wonderful array of color and texture and leaves you with a sense of well-being. Fine Mexican cooking is more than just hot sauce. Using both familiar and nationally distinctive ingredients, it incorporates exciting combinations of spices and sauces, sometimes subtle and complex, sometimes simple and straightforward—but always wonderful to taste and often beautiful to behold.

Growing up in Los Angeles, I could not remain a stranger to Mexican cuisine. I cut my baby teeth on the taquitos from Olvera Street, spent my adolescence among the taco and burrito stands that pepper the landscape, testimony to the rich Latino population here, and ultimately graduated to more sophisticated fare at the better local Mexican restaurants.

However, the most incredible Mexican food in my memory came not from the better restaurants of Mexico City—which usually specialize in Continental cuisine—or from the bustling stands of Olvera Street. It wasn't even found in the popular local restaurants such as Los Arcos or El Adobe, known as the unofficial headquarters

7

of Governor Jerry Brown. It came from the kitchen of my mother's dearest friend, Hélène Juarez.

Hélène is a fifth-generation Californian, educated in Mexico and descended from Cayelano Juarez, who was the patriarch of a fiery land-grant family that settled the Napa Valley in the early 1700s. Her home is filled with beautiful fine art, with simple Mexican folk art, with music, conversation, and most of all with the special tastes and smells of Mexican cuisine.

A meal at Hélène's is always an adventure—for the palate and for the eyes. Served buffet style, in either simple pieces of Mexican pottery bought in Oaxaca and Tijuana, or in treasured and priceless family heirlooms, each meal is a celebration. Whether it is a sumptuous holiday feast of turkey mole, or homemade tamales, or simply a last-minute brunch of Spanish omelettes and tequila sunrises, somehow everything always blends together with the style and spice that permeate her home.

Hélène and I have written this book to help you re-create some of that wonderful ambience in your own home. You may not have five generations of wonderful Spanish heirlooms, but like Hélène you can decorate your table with simple folk pottery or cut tinware, with one or two bright paper flowers, and above all, with food created from the recipes that follow. Authentic at heart, they have been revised and adapted over the years to adjust for what is seasonal, available, and sometimes what is simply and uniquely Hélène's.

Some of the recipes are simple and easy to prepare, though "simple and easy" very often still requires the use of fresh ingredients to achieve the best results. However, there is an ever-increasing variety of canned and pre-packaged sauces and ingredients available in many supermarkets, and while they cannot perfectly substitute for the flavor of fresh ingredients, the results will nonetheless be quite delicious.

Try some of these wonderful dishes. Adjust and change

them to suit your palate and the availability of ingredients, and in no time you will be a true aficionado!
Enjoy!

Paula Holt

NOTE

So that you may share in the growing enthusiasm for Mexican food, we have put together a collection of flavorful and authentic Mexican recipes, *comidas típicas*. Some are simple and some are not.

Mexican cooking is often perceived as elaborate and complicated. And indeed it can be. There is a wonderful feeling of accomplishment when you have roasted and ground up five different varieties of chiles, nuts, seeds, and fresh herbs, and despite the messy kitchen to clean, the results have been worth it! But there are also days when you must produce a good meal without doing much more than opening a small can or jar. The complicated recipes in this book are worth the time, when you have it. But the easy ones are also truly special. And there are now many canned products which can substitute for fresh. Wherever we have felt that commercially prepared ingredients do not impair the dish, we have indicated these time-saving alternatives.

The actual preparation of Mexican food is not really difficult. If you keep the most actively used herbs, spices, and cans of pastes and sauces on your kitchen shelves, and collect a few implements to help you on your way, you will quickly find that there are few national foods that are as much fun to cook and as exciting to eat as Mexican comidas típicas.

H. J.

Authentic Mexican Cooking

CHAPTER I

An Introduction to Mexican Cooking

Kitchen Essentials

Herbs, Spices,
and Special Ingredients

About Chiles

A Word About "Authentic"

A Suggested Shopping List

Kitchen Essentials

Hundreds of years before the blender and the food processor, the Aztecs ground their corn on a *metate* and their chiles on a mortar and pestlelike *molcajete* and *tejolote*, and there are many cooks today who will swear that these ancient implements still do a better job than their modern and elaborate counterparts. If you search out the Mexican and Caribbean stores, in most parts of the country, you will find the above-mentioned primitive and efficient kitchen tools. But you can't be faulted if you prefer to use the time-saving instruments of our technological age.

As my friend, excellent chef and lecturer Philip Brown, says, "In the kitchen, all one needs is one fork and one's fingers." He did add, however, that a whisk might be a help in whipping cream or eggs.

What follows is a list of "essentials," which of course are not at all essential, but will make both the preparation and presentation of Mexican food even more delightful.

A *wooden Mexican bean masher*—Either this or a metal potato masher is helpful, unless you have a strong arm and a wooden spoon.

A *blender*—Two blender jars will make your task lighter and faster.

A *comal*—The *comal* is a round cast-iron griddle with a handle that gets too hot to handle, so keep a potholder nearby. It's a wonderful item to heat tortillas or toast chiles. But you can get by with an easily accessible stove-top griddle and gas flame burners.

Molcajete and tejolote—The Mexican mortar and pestle is the best and most authentic implement for grinding spices and chiles. It works easily for sauces, and can be brought right to the table. The molcajete has been in use for 3,500 years, so we can't put it down for efficiency! It is a round bowl of volcanic rock with three legs, eight inches in diameter and about five inches high. The tejolote, which is the pestle, is best if made from heavy black basalt. The next best is a dark grayish-black stone, which you may be able to find in Mexican markets in the West and Southwest, or at specialty shops throughout the country. If you can't find a molcajete and tejolote, a food processor will do the job.

Tortilla press—Tortilla presses come in two sizes, either four or six inches in diameter. If you can't find ready-made tortillas in your area, you should send for a tortilla press to make the job easier. The only other way to make tortillas is to pat them by hand, or use a rolling pin and roll them out between folds of wax paper. A tortilla press is definitely better.

Cazuelas and ollas—Once you become accustomed to cooking with the Mexican earthenware casseroles and pots, you won't want to use metal or aluminum. They come in a wonderful variety of shapes and sizes, and move beautifully from oven to table, keeping food hot far longer than regular cookware.

With a heat diverter over either electric or gas burners, earthenware casseroles can be used safely on top of the stove. For dishes cooked in an oven, there is never a problem. If you live near a border town, drive down and load up on casseroles of all sizes. They make a Mexican kitchen look wonderful. If you can't find them, use casseroles and baking dishes of flameproof glass.

If you are using the earthenware casseroles and pots, be sure to season them before using, or they can easily crack and give a claylike taste to your food. Fill them almost to the top with warm water (season with oregano, thyme, or bay leaves) and heat them—filled—in a 300° oven for at least four hours. (You will get a better "cure" if you rub the insides of the bowls with garlic before filling with water.)

Herbs, Spices, and Special Ingredients

The piquancy of Mexican cooking depends on herbs, spices, and, of course, chiles. Collect as many of the following as you can and your cooking chores will be simpler. If you can't find them, don't worry: there is always a substitute on your market's spice shelves.

Some of the spices are found throughout the United States in well-known brand names. Others can be found in Mexican, Caribbean, Korean, and Chinese stores.

Look for the following, and if you find them, buy in quantities:

Achiote—A small red seed of the annatto tree. Sometimes marketed under the name "annatto." This seed is used for coloring and flavoring, and lends a color similar to saffron.

Epazote—Packaged in California where it grows wild in the empty lots, epazote is used to flavor many traditional bean and tortilla dishes. Used as an herbal tea, it purportedly does wonders for an upset stomach. Epazote adds a subtle aroma to beans, but you can get along with a touch of oregano, or omit it all together, and still consider yourself an authentic cook.

Cumin—This strongly flavored spice comes in seed and powder form, and is usually mixed with red chiles in commercial chile powders. A common ingredient in Middle Eastern and Spanish cooking as well as Mexican, it adds flavor to enhance the hotness of chiles.

Oregano—An herb beloved in Italy and Spain as well as Mexico, oregano can be found on any spice shelf. It should be rubbed between three fingers and sprinkled over beans, enchiladas, stews, and soups. It frequently appears in its dried form in little bowls on the traditional Mexican table.

Pumpkin Seeds (pepitas)—Pepitas are bottled, salted, and sold throughout the United States to serve with drinks. You should have no trouble finding them in health food stores and specialty food markets. They can be kept indefinitely if stored tightly covered in a dry, cool place. Ground, they make a wonderful addition to sauces for chicken or turkey. Whole, they make a nice garnish to many dishes or can be enjoyed by the handful with your favorite cocktails.

Sesame Seeds—The white ones can be found in Japanese markets, some supermarkets, and specialty food stores. Toast them to a golden-brown and add them to moles. They give a wonderful flavor to dishes with string beans.

Cilantro—Some supermarkets carry this parsleylike herb next to the lettuce or watercress in the fresh produce section. In Chinese markets, you'll find it sold as Chinese parsley. Bright-green, colorful, flavorful, and olorific! Some people hate it, others can't live without it. Spice Islands carries the seeds (coriander) and your local nursery would be likely to carry the fresh herb. It is easy to grow in your own garden and makes a beautiful garnish for many Mexican drinks and dishes. If you bring it home from your local market, it will come with the roots attached. Place it in your refrigerator in a jar of water. It does not keep long, so use it quickly and enjoy it. Full of vitamins!

Dried Shrimp—These can be found in Latin American,

Chinese, and Japanese groceries. In the Mexican specialty sections, you may find them ground, in jars and cans. This is a popular seasoning, used in vegetable dishes and soups.

About Chiles

What gives Mexican food its special individual flavor? Why, the chile pepper, of course. Fresh or dried, there are as many different types of chiles as letters in the alphabet. Some can be found in your local supermarket in the fresh produce bins, others in cans and jars on the shelves, and still others in the dried spice section. A few will have to be searched for or replaced by a more common cousin.

Chile peppers are actually fruits, and more specifically berries. They vary in size, shape, and color from slender and finger-shaped to oval or cone-shaped, from green and yellow to red and purple, from under an inch to over a foot. A good many varieties find their way to the local markets. A limited selection of fresh chiles can be found at most chain groceries and an abundance at smaller Latino markets. You should have little trouble finding at least some varieties of chiles, enough to experiment with most of the recipes that follow. If there are no Mexican groceries in your area, try Korean or Chinese markets where similar spices approximate the Mexican spices. Even for the traditional Mexican cook, all chiles are not available in all regions, and a good Mexican cook has to learn to use whatever is available. A different variety of chile may change the flavor of a dish only slightly, and as you become familiar with the various chiles available, you will be able to substitute one for another. Even within a particular variety of chile, you will find fluctuations in hotness, enough so that quantities indicated in recipes should never be treated as absolutes. Learn to trust your taste buds and palate: they are your best flavor guides.

For recipes calling for fresh green chiles, you may have to substitute the canned California chiles or chiles verdes, even though the recipe has specified a poblano or pasilla chile. You may use jalapeños when it calls for serrano, or vice versa, and if neither is available, you may have to use crushed cayenne pepper. Even a dash of Tabasco sauce—which is made from the capsicum pepper—will give you the bite if not the total flavor.

Here is a handful of the better-known chiles, both the fresh green (unripened) chiles, and the dried red (ripened) chiles. Don't be confused by the fact that the same chile will appear in both forms, for the long green tapering California chile, which you will stuff for a chile relleno, is dried to a red powder and becomes California chili powder; and the beautiful dark-green pasilla dries to the hot woodsy-tasting red pasilla.

Fresh Chiles

Chiles Verdes—Also known as California chiles, these are the long and tapered green chiles, with a light-green, shiny surface. They are fairly mild, especially with the seeds and membranes removed, and are used extensively in a variety of dishes. Chiles verdes, or green chiles, or California chiles (or Anaheim chiles!) are readily available in cans, either whole or diced. These are the chiles traditionally used in chiles rellenos. You could substitute a green, unripened pasilla chile or ancho chile, though the ancho chile tends to be a little hotter to the taste.

Chiles Poblanos—Darker green and plumper than the chiles verdes, the poblanos are deliciously mild and are wonderful stuffed with meat or cheese. They are similar to regular bell peppers, and you could substitute with other varieties, but the results would not be as flavorful.

To use fresh green chiles, first fire roast them. Place the chile directly over a gas flame until the skin blisters. If you do not have a gas burner, you can char them under a broiler or in a very hot oven. When they blister, wrap them in wet paper towels until they are cool enough to handle. The skins should come off easily. Remove the seeds and membranes, and you have a mild, flavorful chile. Some cooks prefer to soak a chile in water with a teaspoon of vinegar to reduce the bite.

Jalapeños—These come in many colors, depending on the season—red, green, or yellow; small and puffy; and sometimes fire hot. Jalapeños are about two inches long and blimp-shaped, and are prepared with or without the seeds and membranes according to the hotness desired. They are widely distributed in fresh or canned form, and also available pickled (*en escabeche*). Pickled jalapeños are wonderful as garnishes, but in cooking will alter the flavor of the finished dish.

Serranos—Used in Northern Chinese and Szechuan as well as in Mexican cooking, serrano chiles, found fresh or in cans, are slightly smaller than jalapeños and are quite hot. To reduce the hotness, remove the membranes and seeds and rinse in cold water before using.

Dried Chiles

In Mexico, the dried red chiles are often soaked in water overnight to soften them before they are added to other ingredients. You can simply cover them with water in a saucepan, bring the water to a boil, and let the chiles soak until softened (10–15 minutes). To puree for use in sauces, remove the stems and seeds and process in a blender with just enough water to make a paste. You may want to go the extra step of pressing the puree through a sieve to remove any peel and make a smoother puree.

If you are replacing whole dried chiles in a recipe with a commercial powder, allow about one tablespoon of dried chili powder for each large (ancho or pasilla) chile. Try to find the pure ground chili, since most commercial powders are a mixture of various chiles, cumin, oregano, and garlic, and the flavors will not substitute perfectly.

Although most national-brand chili powders will read chili powder or "red chili pepper," there are several smaller companies that package pure pasilla, ancho, California, or New Mexico chiles, and it is well worth your while to seek them out. They will give you much greater control over flavor balance than blended chili powders.

Here are a few of the better-known dried chiles:

California or Anaheim Chiles—These are large and smooth-skinned with a dark-red color. They are fairly mild. You may find a similar chile labeled "New Mexico" chile, which is slightly hotter to the taste.

Pasilla Chiles—The ripened version of the pasilla chile is dark-red and gently hot with a rich, woodsy flavor.

Ancho Chiles—These are orange-red in color and can sometimes be very hot.

Mulato Chiles—Darker than the ancho and slightly more biting in taste.

Guajillo Chiles—Long and narrow and light-red in color; smooth-skinned and fairly hot.

Chiles Negros—This chile is almost black and varies in hotness, but has a distinctive flavor all its own.

Chiles Pequins—About the size of a pumpkin seed, these are used in sauces or ground flavorings. Simply crumble in your fingers before adding to sauces or other dishes. Use judiciously, as these are fairly hot.

Chiles Tepins—Bright-red dried pods, some shaped like small red balls resembling a Spanish peanut. But don't eat them by the handfuls—hot, hot, hot!

Chipotle Chiles—These are often found canned or pickled in a marinade, and have a distinctively smoky flavor. (*Morita chiles* are smaller but almost identical in taste to the chipotle—also found pickled, the two varieties can be used interchangeably.)

Remember that handling chiles can be a searing experience and requires some caution. Once you start working with them, do not rub your eyes. The volatile oils can sting your skin and burn your eyes and lips, and some cooks actually prefer working with thin rubber gloves when they are using particularly hot chiles. In all chiles, it is the seeds and internal membranes that are the hottest and most irritating, and these are usually discarded before cooking.

The chiles not only burn fingers, but have healing qualities as well, an abundance of vitamins A, B, and E, and more vitamin C than an orange! People of tropical climates savor the hotness of the peppers, because when eaten they tend to cool the body, while at the same time, they quicken the blood.

No authentic Mexican table is complete without a basket of chiles—fresh, or blended into a piquant sauce with tomatoes and onions, and spiced with the dried aromatic leaves of oregano.

Not everyone can take the fire and spice of authentic Mexican cookery. The recipes included, especially the sauces, have in many cases been toned down to suit the Anglo palate. Nevertheless, chiles can be unpredictable and you may want to make adjustments.

If, for example, your taste decrees that the sauce

should be hotter than our recipes indicate, add another chile or two or include some of the fiery seeds. But if by chance you overdo the spices, you can tone the dish down by adding a potato, a ground-up tortilla, or a ground-up French roll.

A Word or Two About "Authentic"

If you are preparing an *authentic* Mexican meal, you will probably be using lard for frying. There is no substitute for the flavor, but for some dishes you may prefer the lighter touch of sweet butter or vegetable oil.

Authentic Mexican soups are actually made from a water-based stock; however this is more a matter of economy than of taste. That is why we have included the double beef broth and double chicken broth. Authentic? No, but much better.

Another authentic budget-stretcher is the addition of potatoes to tacos, and many of the local stands on Olvera Street do just that. The potatoes have a nice flavor, but they do make the taco filling starchier.

In Mexico, food and drink are often garnished with a slice of *limón*, which is really not a lemon but a lime. Limes add a distinctive flavor and make a prettier garnish than lemons, but are not always available and can be rather costly. It is the authentic way to go, but a lemon will often do.

Following is a list of special ingredients for Mexican cooking:

Mexican Chocolate—Mexican chocolate can be found in all Latin groceries and most specialty shops. It is a semi-sweet chocolate flavored with cinnamon. If you cannot

easily find the authentic variety, use any semisweet chocolate and add a sprinkling of cinnamon and a touch of
vanilla to it.

Chorizo—This hot Spanish or Mexican sausage can be
found in cans imported from Spain and is also made
locally in many markets and sold in the fresh meat de-
partments. We have included two recipes for homemade
chorizo on pages 116 and 117, which are somewhat more
refined and less greasy than the commercially packaged
variety.

Crema—A cross between commercial sour cream and the
more delicate *creme fraîche, crema* is lighter and less acid
tasting than the commercial sour creams. It is easy to
make at home; simply add a few tablespoons of buttermilk to a half-pint of whipping cream and let stand unrefrigerated for a few hours. Stir and refrigerate, and it
will thicken to a beautifully rich, slightly sour cream that
will stay in the refrigerator for about a week or 10 days.

Jicama—You may not yet be familiar with this crunchy,
somewhat sweet white turnip, which you will find in your
produce department hiding inside an ugly stringy brown
skin. Crisp but bland until you sprinkle it with chili pepper and lime juice. Then it's delicious.

Tomato Puree—When a recipe calls for tomato puree, I
prefer the use of blanched, chopped, and seeded fresh
tomatoes. Two medium-sized tomatoes yield about one
cup of fresh tomato puree. Blanching allows the skins to
be removed with little difficulty, and is done by dropping
tomatoes into boiling water for 45 seconds to 1 minute.

Mexican Vanilla—If you live near a border town, stock
up on the pure Mexican vanilla extract, which is far more

flavorful than the commercial vanilla extract available here and certainly cheaper than using fresh vanilla beans.

Tomatillos—These are small firm green tomatolike vegetables, covered with a papery husk that is removed before cooking. Tomatillos have a distinctive acid flavor and are excellent in green sauces for chicken and enchilada dishes. They are available fresh in some produce sections, and in canned form are widely distributed.

A Suggested Shopping List

Chiles

The essential—the indispensable—chiles should always be on hand like a handy supply of stamps. When you find them, buy as many of the canned, powdered, and dried varieties as you can store.

Dried Chiles (whole and in powdered form):
    Pasilla chiles
    California (Anaheim) chiles
    Ancho chiles
    Guajillo chiles

Canned (Green) Chiles:
    Four-ounce cans fire-roasted green chiles, whole and
        diced
    Seven-ounce cans fire-roasted green chiles, whole
    Jalapeños chiles en escabeche (hot pickled chiles)

Spices

Achiote (annatto)
Anise
Cinnamon
Cloves, whole
Oregano
Coriander seed
Cayenne

Cumin
Peppercorns
Oregano
Epazote (if you can find it!)
Thyme
Marjoram
Paprika

Nuts and Seeds

Almonds, blanched and unblanched
Pumpkin seeds (pepitas)
Sesame seeds

Cans and Jars

Tomatillos enteros (whole tomatillos)
Whole tomatoes
Pimientos
Green olives, pitted
Black olives
Mild white vinegar
Peanut oil
Capers
Hominy

Also on Hand

Quaker Oats masa harina
Long-grain white rice
Pounds of lard
Mexican chocolate (Ibarra)
Raisins and currants
Packages of corn husks (for tamales)

Fresh Produce
That You Will Want to Seek Out

Cilantro
Fresh pasilla chiles
Fresh California chiles
Fresh serrano chiles
Jicama
Fresh tomatillos

CHAPTER II

Sauces

Mexican food is not just tacos and beans, nor is it food so hot that you can't taste it. The sauces (*salsas*) give a variety of flavors to many dishes, and allow for degrees of "hot" from mild to fiery. Typically, a table is set with a choice of three salsas—one very mild, one spiced with some chile, and one that is not for the faint of heart.

Salsa cruda, salsa fresca, and salsa picante are all fresh (uncooked) sauces, varying in hotness and spiciness according to the kinds and amounts of chiles used. The fresh sauces have a very short shelf-life; however, if you heat your remaining sauce in olive oil, it turns into a cooked sauce, which can remain in your refrigerator for up to a week and still retain its flavor.

Salsa fogata, salsa de chile pasilla, salsa roja, salsa campesina, and the various moles—sauces made from the pulp of dried red chiles—can be made in advance and kept frozen.

Salsa Cruda

Mild Tomato Sauce for Tacos

2 *ripe tomatoes, peeled, seeded, and chopped*
1 *(7-oz.) can diced green chiles*
1 *small onion, finely chopped*
Salt to taste
Fresh ground pepper
Pinch sugar
1 *tablespoon fresh cilantro*

Mix all ingredients except cilantro. Let stand for at least 1 hour until flavors mix. Add cilantro and serve as a cold garnish for cooked meats, poultry, tacos, and tostados.

Makes 1½ cups.

Salsa Fresca

Fresh Sauce

3 *medium-ripe tomatoes, peeled, seeded, and chopped*
½ *cup finely chopped onion*
1 *jalapeño chile, seeded, finely chopped*
1 *tablespoon olive oil*
1 *teaspoon vinegar*
1 *teaspoon lime juice*
½ *teaspoon oregano*
Salt to taste

Combine tomatoes, onion, and chile in a mixing bowl. Add olive oil, vinegar, lime juice, oregano, and salt. Let stand unrefrigerated until flavors blend (about 1 hour). Serve with tacos or as a garnish for meats.

Makes 2 cups.

Fresh sauces will keep only a short time in your refrigerator. If you have sauce left, heat a teaspoon of oil in a small saucepan and cook the sauce, stirring constantly, for a few moments. Cooked and refrigerated, it will last for over a week.

Salsa Picante

Red Tomato Sauce

> 2 *fresh jalapeño chiles, with stems*
> *and membranes removed (seeded*
> *for a milder sauce, seeds left in for*
> *more bite)*
> 1 *clove garlic*
> 4 *ripe tomatoes, peeled, seeded, and*
> *chopped*
> 2 *scallions, finely chopped—whites*
> *and greens*
> ½ *teaspoon oregano*
> ¾ *cup water*
> *Salt to taste*
> 2 *tablespoons chopped cilantro*
> *Juice of 1 lime*

In a processor or blender, finely chop chiles and garlic. Place in a mixing bowl. Add tomatoes, scallions, oregano, and water. Stir until flavors are mixed. Add salt to taste.

Stir in the chopped cilantro and lime juice and serve. (If made in advance, mix all ingredients except cilantro and lime juice, which should be added immediately before serving.)

Makes 4 cups.

Mantequilla de Pobre

Poor Man's Butter

> 2 *medium-sized avocados*
> 2 *tomatoes, blanched and peeled*
> 1 *tablespoon salad oil*
> 2 *tablespoons wine vinegar*
> *Salt*

Dice avocados and tomatoes into little cubes. Add oil, vinegar, and salt to taste.

Toss gently and serve as a garnish for rice, or with meat or chicken.

Makes about 2 cups.

Salsa de Guacamole

Guacamole Sauce for Taquitos

> 2 *tablespoons pepitas (pumpkin seeds)*
> 1 *(3-oz.) can green peeled chiles*
> ¾ *cup parsley*
> ⅓ *cup chicken broth*
> ¼ *cup oil*
> 2 *ripe avocados*

Grind pepitas with chiles and parsley in a blender or food processor. When finely ground, add a little chicken broth and strain through a fine sieve. Add the strained mixture and remaining broth to hot oil and heat thoroughly. When cool, add mashed avocados and stir until smooth. (For a smoother sauce, return broth mixture and avocados to food processor and process with on/off motion until smooth.)

Makes 2 cups.

Salsa Ranchera

Ranch-Style Sauce with Tomatoes and Chiles

This salsa is a wonderful garnish for tacos or tostadas, slightly hotter in taste than the salsa cruda.

> 2 tomatoes, peeled
> ¼ cup chopped onion
> 1 clove garlic
> 1 canned jalapeño chile (pickled)
> 1 teaspoon olive oil
> ¼ teaspoon oregano
> ¼ teaspoon salt

In a blender or food processor, combine tomatoes, onion, garlic, and chile. Blend until fairly smooth. Heat oil in a small pan and add tomato mixture. Season with oregano and salt. Bring to a boil and simmer gently for about 10 minutes. Remove from heat and let stand until flavors mingle—about 2 hours.

Makes about 1 cup.

Salsa Fogata

Hot Chile Sauce

> 2–3 dried hot red chile peppers (pasilla
>   or ancho), or ½ cup tepins,
>   cayenne, or guajillo
> 2   cups tomato juice
> 3   tablespoons cider vinegar
> 4   cloves garlic
> ½   teaspoon oregano
> ¼   teaspoon sugar
> ¼   teaspoon salt

Remove ends from chiles and discard. Soak in hot water to soften. Place chiles in blender or food processor, along with 1 cup tomato juice, the cider vinegar, garlic, and oregano. Process until garlic and chiles are finely chopped. Add remaining tomato juice and blend. Add sugar to cut acidity of tomato, and salt.

Place in a tightly covered jar and refrigerate. Will keep about a week.

Makes 2½ cups.

Salsa de Chile Pasilla

Pasilla Chile Sauce for Meat or Chicken

> 6   dried pasilla chiles
> 1   clove garlic
> ¾   cup cold water
> 1   tomato, peeled and seeded
> ½   teaspoon salt

Toast chiles on a warm griddle or comal, or in a heavy ungreased skillet. In a blender combine garlic, chiles, water, tomato, and salt. Blend together until smooth. This subtly flavored sauce is wonderful served with chicken, with meats, or on huevos rancheros.

Makes about 2 cups.

Note: If this sauce is too piquant for your taste, remove the seeds and veins from the chiles before toasting.

Salsa Roja

Red Chile Sauce for Enchiladas

8 *ancho chiles, dried (for a milder*
  sauce, use California or pasilla
  chiles)
2 *cloves garlic*
1 *medium-sized onion, chopped*
¼ *cup cooking oil*
Salt to taste
Red vinegar (optional)
¼ *teaspoon cumin*

Soak chiles overnight in water. Remove chiles, but save the liquid. Devein, remove stems and seeds.

In a blender, chop garlic and onion. Add chiles and about ¼ cup of the liquid they were soaked in. Blend until pureed to a smooth sauce.

In a saucepan or skillet, heat oil and add pureed sauce. Cook until oil is absorbed into the sauce. Taste and correct seasoning by adding salt or a touch of red vinegar.

Add cumin. Use salsa roja with chicken, meat, or cheese enchiladas.

Makes enough for 12 enchiladas.

Note: For a slightly mellower sauce, add ¼ cup tomato sauce in place of the chile liquid.

Salsa de Chile en Polvo

Sauce for Enchiladas Made from
Chili Powder

This is a good substitute for salsa roja if you have trouble finding dried chiles.

> 3 tablespoons vegetable oil
> 2 tablespoons flour
> ¼ cup California red chili powder
> 2 cups beef broth
> 2 (10½-oz.) cans tomato puree
> ½ teaspoon oregano
> ¼ teaspoon cumin
> ¼ teaspoon garlic powder
> Salt to taste

In a large saucepan, heat oil. Stir in flour and cook for about 1 minute, or until flour is no longer raw. Add chili powder and beef broth. Continue stirring. Add tomato puree, oregano, cumin, and garlic powder. Taste and correct seasoning, adding salt if needed.

Simmer on a low flame for about 15–20 minutes.

Makes enough sauce for 12 enchiladas.

Salsa de Tomatillo (or Salsa Verde)

Green Tomatillo Sauce

1½ pounds fresh tomatillos, or
1 (13-oz.) can tomatillos, drained
1 small onion, chopped
2 serrano chiles or other hot green
chiles, seeded and deveined, or
1 small can mild green chiles
1 clove garlic
½ cup chicken broth
½ teaspoon salt
Pepper
2 tablespoons olive oil

If using fresh tomatillos, remove husks. Wash off the sticky residue in cold water. Cut tomatillos in half. Place in a saucepan and cover with water. Add onions, chiles, and garlic and boil until tender, about 8 minutes. Drain.

Place tomatillo mixture in a blender or food processor and puree. Thin with chicken broth if too thick. Season with salt and pepper to taste.

Heat oil in a skillet and add sauce. Cook for about 5 minutes, stirring constantly.

Sauce may be stored in an air-tight container for about 3 weeks. Excellent on enchiladas!

Makes 2½–3 cups.

Salsa Campesina

Country-Style Sauce

On ranches, this piquant sauce—an adobo—*would be made with chiles steeped in pulque, a powerful liquor made from the juice of the maguey. Here we can substitute tequila or gin. Once when out of both, I tried Stolichnaya vodka, and it was heavenly! Serve salsa campesina with chicken, with pork, or with bits of lamb made into an empanada.*

> 2 *dried ancho chiles*
> 4 *dried pasilla chiles*
> 2 *tablespoons olive oil or peanut oil*
> 1 *clove garlic, minced*
> ¼ *cup tequila, gin, or vodka*

Wash, devein, and seed the chiles. Place them in boiling water, turn off the heat, and let them steep for 30 minutes. Drain. Heat oil and fry chiles, along with the garlic. Place in a blender or food processor and blend to a smooth paste. Add the liquor and continue to blend until absorbed.

This sauce will keep in the refrigerator for a week without losing its zest. It can be frozen.

Makes 1–1½ cups.

Salsa de Chile Cascabel

Cascabel Chile Sauce (Medium-Hot)

This is a perfect taco sauce for those who want something stronger than a simple salsa cruda.

> 6 dried cascabel chiles (the long red
> Japanese peppers can be used if you
> cannot find cascabels)
> 2 tomatoes, peeled and seeded
> 3 cloves garlic
> ½ teaspoon salt
> ½ cup (or less) water

Toast chiles on a comal or ungreased heavy skillet, turning constantly so that they do not burn. When they are cool enough to handle, slit them open and remove veins and seeds. For a hotter sauce, separate the seeds and toast separately, stirring so that they don't burn. Broil tomatoes briefly. Place chiles (with or without seeds), broiled tomatoes, garlic, and salt in your blender and combine until smooth, adding water if needed.

Makes 1½–2 cups.

Mole Sencillo

Easy Mole Sauce

For a mole sauce without the fuss, try this easier version:

> 2 cloves garlic, finely minced
> 4 tablespoons oil
> 3 tablespoons peanut butter
> 1 (3-oz.) can mole poblano (powder) or
> an equivalent jar of moist mole
> sauce
> 3 cups chicken broth

Simmer garlic in oil for a few seconds. Then add peanut butter and stir until well mixed. Add the dry mole powder or the mole sauce and continue stirring over a low flame until blended. Slowly add the broth and keep stirring until sauce is the consistency of a puree. (Sauce can be thinned with more broth or thickened with 2 tablespoons of flour in ½ cup of cold water.)

Makes about 3 cups.

Mole Poblano

Mole Sauce with Four Kinds of Chiles

Each variety of dried chile adds to the flavor of this mole sauce, which is wonderful with either chicken or turkey. Be sure to make enough additional to use as a sauce for enchiladas.

> 2 pasilla chiles
> 2 ancho chiles
> 2 New Mexico chiles
> 2 California chiles
> ¼ cup peanuts, or 2 tablespoons
>   peanut butter
> ¼ cup blanched almonds, slivered
> ⅛ cup sesame seeds
> ¼ tablet Mexican chocolate, or
>   1 ounce semisweet chocolate and
>   ¼ teaspoon ground cinnamon
> 3 cloves garlic, minced
> ½ onion, chopped
> 2 tablespoons oil
> 4 cups chicken broth
> Pinch oregano
> Pinch ground cumin
> 1 tomato, peeled and chopped

Toast the chiles 15 minutes in an ungreased skillet, then soak for 15 minutes in boiling water. Drain. Remove seeds and stems. Grind in blender or food processor with either a little chicken broth or water from the chiles to facilitate grinding. When smooth, strain the mixture through a coarse sieve to remove any bits of peel.

Grind together peanuts, almonds, sesame seeds, and chocolate with minced garlic and chopped onion. Simmer mixture in 2 tablespoons of oil until the onion and garlic are translucent, but do not brown. Add 2 cups of the broth, oregano, cumin, and tomato, and cook for 15 minutes. Add the chile pulp and stir until blended. You may want to run mixture through blender or processor again to get a smoother puree. Return mixture to cooking pot and add additional 2 cups of broth. Cook slowly over a low flame for about 30 minutes. Will keep refrigerated for about a week.

Makes enough for 2 chickens or 12 enchiladas.

🔲🔲🔲🔲🔲🔲🔲🔲🔲🔲🔲🔲🔲🔲🔲🔲🔲🔲🔲🔲🔲🔲🔲🔲🔲🔲🔲🔲

CHAPTER III

Appetizers and Snacks

🔲🔲🔲🔲🔲🔲🔲🔲🔲🔲🔲🔲🔲🔲🔲🔲🔲🔲🔲🔲🔲🔲🔲🔲🔲🔲🔲🔲

Totopas

Tortilla Chips

Yes, you can go to your grocer's shelf and buy a bag of ready-made tortilla chips, but just as the canned salsas cannot really taste the same as your own freshly made with ripe tomatoes, fresh onions, and cilantro, so the ready-made tortilla chips cannot hold a candle to the ones you can cook up in a matter of a few minutes.

Serve fresh totopas to accompany guacamole, or set them out in a basket accompanied by a red salsa cruda, a salsa verde, and a small bowl of sour cream for dipping.

Grate cheddar or Monterey Jack cheese over a plate of totopas and heat until the cheese melts for delicious nachos (easily made in a microwave, and a favorite with hungry after-school children). Flavor the nachos with diced green chiles (canned are fine) or top with sliced black olives, sour cream, or guacamole—or all three!

> 6 tortillas (or however many you need)
> Oil for frying

Cut tortillas into 8 wedges, or 6 if you want a bigger dipping chip. Tortillas can be stacked and cut with a sharp heavy knife (a Chinese cleaver is terrific) to save time.

Heat enough oil in a saucepan to give you 2–3 inches, and drop in tortilla chips, careful not to crowd the pan. Remove chips as they become crisp and golden and drain on paper towels.

Note: If your tortillas are not fresh off the comal, make a light saltwater solution and brush salt water lightly on both sides of the tortilla, using your hands or a small pastry brush. Either blot or let dry before frying to prevent oil from spattering. The water freshens up a slightly stale tortilla. The salt in the water is for flavor.

Guacamole

Avocado Dip

To make a spicier guacamole, add 1 chopped fresh or canned jalapeño pepper.

> 4 ripe avocados
> 1 ripe tomato, peeled and seeded
> ¼ cup finely chopped onion
> 1 teaspoon oregano
> Juice ½ lemon
> Salt to taste
> ¼ cup chopped fresh cilantro
> (optional)

Mash avocados with a fork until a paste is formed. Chop tomatoes and add to avocados. Stir in onion, oregano, and lemon juice until thoroughly blended. Add salt to taste, and cilantro (optional). To make blending easier, you might add a dash of cold water.

Refrigerate mixture, covered, for about 30 minutes before serving.

To prevent avocado from turning brown, place seed in the guacamole and remove just before serving. Serve with fresh totopas.

Makes 4 cups.

Chile con Queso

Chile with Cheese

> 2 tablespoons vegetable oil
> 1 clove garlic, minced
> 1 medium-sized onion, chopped
> 2 medium-sized tomatoes, peeled, seeded, and chopped
> 1 (4-oz.) can diced green chiles, or 3 fresh California chiles, roasted
> 2 jalapeño (or serrano) chiles, roasted, peeled, and chopped
> 8 ounces Monterey Jack cheese, shredded
> 8 ounces cheddar cheese, shredded
> 1 cup sour cream

Heat oil in a large saucepan. Add garlic and onions and cook until translucent but not browned. Add tomatoes and stir. Add chiles, finely chopped, and continue stirring. Add cheese and cook over a low heat, stirring constantly, until cheese has melted. Stir in sour cream and continue cooking just until heated through.

Serve in a chafing dish with fresh totopas.

Makes about 4 cups.

Mexican Pizza

Place a large flour tortilla on a baking sheet. Top with ground beef that has been browned with onions and diced green chiles. Top with a layer of grated Monterey Jack cheese. Cut into wedges and serve as an appetizer, after you have placed it under a hot broiler long enough to melt cheese.

Tortilla con Queso

Place a large flour tortilla on a baking sheet. Top with a combination of grated Monterey Jack and cheddar cheeses. Add sliced jalapeño peppers and broil until cheese melts and tortilla is crisp at the edges.

Nachos

Place a mound of tortilla chips (see totopas–p. 42) on oven-proof dish. Top with grated cheddar cheese (or a mixture of cheddar and Monterey Jack). Use lots of cheese! Add slices of jalapeño peppers and place under a broiler until cheese melts.

Serve with salsa, guacamole, and sour cream.

Carnitas #1

Little Meat Cubes

Served in the men-only cantinas! No reason to deny these to the women.

> 2 pounds lean pork
> Salt and pepper to taste
> A dusting of pasilla pepper, ground

Cut the pork into 1-inch cubes. Dust with salt, pepper, and pasilla pepper, and let rest for 1 hour.

Place the meat in a shallow baking pan in a 300° oven for about 2 hours. Pour or siphon off the fat from time to time. Drain on paper towels and serve.

Makes 25–30 carnitas.

Note: Delicious served with poor man's butter (see page 31), guacamole (see page 31), or salsa cruda (see page 29). Better yet, serve all 3 and let your guests choose.

Carnitas #2

Little Meat Cubes

These carnitas are a touch sweeter than the previous recipe. They are delicious served with warmed corn tortillas and a selection of salsas—salsa cruda, salsa tomatillo, and salsa picante.

¼ cup lard or vegetable oil
1 clove garlic, minced
*2 pounds lean boneless pork butt, cut
    into 1-inch cubes*
Salt to taste
Paprika
½ cup fresh orange juice

Heat the oil or lard in a large, heavy Dutch oven until almost smoking. Add minced garlic. Spread the pork over the bottom and season with salt and paprika to taste. Reduce heat to medium and sauté until meat is golden on all sides—15–20 minutes. Do not crowd pan. (You may have to sauté meat in two batches.)

When meat has been sautéed, remove with a slotted spoon, and pour off fat. Return meat to Dutch oven and add orange juice. Stir frequently over a high heat until boiling. Reduce heat and simmer, uncovered, until liquid is thickened, and orange juice has formed a glaze on the pork—about 10–12 minutes.

Cover and bake in a preheated 300° oven until meat is very tender—about 30 minutes.

Makes 25–30 Carnitas.

Carne Cocida en Limón

Steak Tartar with Lime

> ½ pound ground sirloin, very lean
> ½ cup lime juice
> 1 small tomato, finely chopped
> 2 tablespoons finely chopped onions
> 3 serrano chiles, finely chopped
> Salt to taste

Mix the lime juice into the ground meat and set aside in the refrigerator for 6 hours. Add the rest of the ingredients, mix well, and set in refrigerator for 2 more hours. Serve with totopos or crisply fried tortillas.

Serves 4 as appetizer.

Coctel de Abulón

Abalone Cocktail

For this use canned abalone, available in most markets everywhere. Cut the meat in cubes, add its own juices, and season with lemon or lime to taste. Top with a fresh sauce of tomatoes, oregano, green onions, cilantro, and minced jalapeño peppers, or salsa picante (see p. 30).

Camarónes al Barbacoa
Barbecued Shrimp

You've never tasted a better hors d'oeuvre than shrimp marinated for a short time and tossed on the barbecue grill before you start your steaks.

> 1 *dozen large shrimp or prawns,*
>   *uncooked with shells on*
> 2 *lemons*
> ¼ *cup olive oil*
> *Salt to taste*
> *Dash flaked red pepper*
> *Dash sherry (optional)*

Butterfly the shrimps (slit down the spine and clean, removing vein). Leave the tails and a little shell above them. Marinate in the juice of 2 lemons, olive oil, salt, and a few flakes of red pepper. If you wish, add a touch of sherry to the marinade. When the coals are ready, toss the shrimp on the grate, turning once or twice, until they just turn pink. Do not overcook. When they are cool enough to handle, eat them with your fingers.

Serves 4 as appetizer.

Coctel de Jaiba o Camarón
Shrimp or Crab Cocktail

> ½ pound small Iceland shrimp, or ½
>   pound shredded crabmeat
> Juice of 3 limes or 2 lemons
> ⅛ cup olive oil
> 1 medium-sized tomato, peeled,
>   seeded, and finely chopped
> 1 green onion, finely chopped
> 1 cucumber, peeled, seeded, and
>   finely chopped
> 1 serrano chile, finely chopped
> ½ head iceberg lettuce, finely
>   shredded
> Catsup (optional)
> Cilantro, several fresh sprigs

Marinate shrimp or crab in lemon or lime juice and olive oil while you are chopping the vegetables. Combine seafood, tomato, onion, and cucumber. Add chile and stir.

When serving, place the shredded lettuce at the bottom of a cocktail dish (you can always use a large wineglass if you don't have the perfect cocktail dish). Add the shrimp or crab mixture. If you are a devotee of catsup, add it to taste.

Serve with a last-minute topping of salsa cruda (see pg. 29) and a few sprigs of cilantro.

Serves 4–6.

Ceviche

Fresh Seafood Cocktail

> 1 *pound white fish (red snapper, bass,*
> *any firm-fleshed fish, or scallops), cut*
> *into cubes*
> *Juice of 2 lemons or 3 limes*
> 2 *tomatoes, blanched, peeled, and chopped*
> 1 *jalapeño pepper, diced*
> 2 *serrano chiles, finely chopped*
> 2 *green onions, finely minced*
> *Capers*
> *Olive oil*
> *Cilantro or parsley, a few fresh sprigs*
> *Salt to taste*

Cut fish into cubes or slice scallops. Let them marinate overnight in the juice of lemons or limes. In the morning, pour off the liquid and reserve. Place the marinated fish, tomatoes, peppers, onions, and capers in a mixing bowl. Mix the reserved liquid with a tablespoon or 2 of olive oil, and pour over the fish. Sprinkle with chopped parsley or cilantro.

Stir and chill. Taste, and add salt, if desired.

Serve as an appetizer or first course in individual cocktail dishes or from a crystal bowl.

Serves 4.

Note: For a deluxe addition, at the last minute add cubes of avocado and slices of lime.

When fresh squid is available, it can be used in the preceding recipe, either alone or mixed with scallops and fresh fish. Have your fish market clean the squid. Cut it into rings and substitute squid for scallops or combine them. Delicious!

Chiles Rellenos
con Jaiba y Camarón

Stuffed Chiles with Shrimp and Crab

The lovely small yellow chiles available in most super-markets can be slit, blanched for seconds, and cooled, then stuffed with a mixture of seafood and displayed on a bed of Boston or butter lettuce. Beautiful as an appetizer or when served as a salad.

> 12 small yellow chiles (guero or wax chiles)
> 1 tablespoon vinegar
> ½ pound crabmeat or small shrimp, or combination
> 2 scallions, minced
> ½ cup mayonnaise
> Juice ½ lemon
> 2 pickled jalapeño peppers, minced

Slit the chiles and remove seeds and veins. Blanch quickly in water with 1 tablespoon of vinegar (about 1 minute). Drain and cool.

In the food processor, or by hand if you prefer, finely chop the shrimps and crabmeat. Mix in the minced scallions and mayonnaise. Sprinkle with lemon juice and stir again.

Stuff the chiles with the seafood mixture and arrange on a plate. If serving as a salad, place 3–4 stuffed chiles on a bed of lettuce. As an hors d'oeuvre, arrange on an attractive serving plate and add a garnish of jalapeño chile on the side.

Serves 6.

Fresh Vegetable Basket

If you are planning an elaborate Mexican meal or grand buffet dinner, it is always nice to offer a selection of fresh vegetables as a light appetizer and let your guests save their appetites for the wonders to come. If you lack the perfect platter or basket, here's a beautiful first-course presentation.

Have your produce man save you the largest and most attractive savoy cabbage available. (They are not available year-round in all parts of the country, but you can ask in advance or place a special order.) The cabbage is your serving dish. Open the cabbage carefully, but do not separate leaves from base. Cut out the very center of the cabbage and insert a small bowl filled with your favorite dipping sauce. Between each of the larger leaves, arrange thin-sliced carrot sticks, celery sticks, radishes, cucumbers, green and red bell pepper strips, and jicama sticks. (Jicama is a bland white turnip with a sweet, crispy taste. It is better with a squeeze of lime and a sprinkling of chili powder.)

Serve as an appetizer, or make it the colorful centerpiece of your buffet table.

CHAPTER IV

⊞⊞⊞⊞⊞⊞⊞⊞⊞⊞⊞⊞⊞⊞⊞⊞⊞⊞⊞⊞⊞⊞⊞⊞⊞⊞⊞⊞

Soups (Wet Soups)

⊞⊞⊞⊞⊞⊞⊞⊞⊞⊞⊞⊞⊞⊞⊞⊞⊞⊞⊞⊞⊞⊞⊞⊞⊞⊞⊞⊞

This chapter deals with "wet" soups—soups as we know them—which are liquid and served at the beginning of a meal. In Mexican cuisine, there is also a "dry" soup, a *sopa seca*, which is made of rice or noodles cooked in soup stock until the stock is completely absorbed.

The soups of Mexico are flavorful and piquant, but often too thin for American taste. The reason is that most soups are *caldos de pobres*, poor men's soups, which call for water instead of a fortified broth. The remedy: A double chicken or beef broth, which can make nectar out of a caldo de pobre, turning it into a rich man's soup.

They are also excellent in all recipes where a broth is called for, and can be made in advance and stored in your freezer. Of course, if you have none on hand, you can substitute a good canned broth.

Caldo de Rez Especial

Double-Rich Beef Broth

>   1½ pounds beef chuck or brisket to
>   each quart cold water
>   4–6 oxtails
>   2 cloves garlic
>   1 onion
>   1 bay leaf
>   1 branch celery with leaves
>   1 whole onion stuck with cloves
>   1 teaspoon thyme
>   1 teaspoon oregano
>   Salt to taste

For a brown broth, sear the meat in a small amount of oil. Otherwise bring to a boil and skim constantly to remove the gray scum. When the broth is clear, add the vegetables, herbs, and salt, and simmer, covered, for 3 hours. Remove the meat and skim the fat. Strain and cook down for 30 minutes without a cover.

(The meat can be used for tacos, burritos, picadillo, or in hearty soups.)

Makes 3–4 cups.

Caldo de Pollo Especial

Double-Rich Chicken Broth

> 1 large stewing hen, plus 3 pounds
>   extra chicken backs and necks
> Salt to taste
> 1 onion
> 1 small carrot
> 1 bay leaf
> 1–2 leeks

Add 1 quart cold water to each 1½ pounds chicken and bring slowly to the boiling point; then skim. Add salt, onion, carrot, bay leaf, and leeks. Cover and simmer for 2 hours. Then cook for another hour, uncovered, so that the liquid cooks down. If you wish to use the chicken in other dishes, you can remove it at this time and add a can of chicken broth. Cool and refrigerate. Skim off the chilled fat and strain the broth.

Sopa de Albóndigas

Meat Ball Soup

If you load the broth with tiny meat balls, you won't need an entree. If you just add 2 or 3 balls to the broth, you have a nice opener for a Mexican comida.

The Broth:
> 6 tomatoes
> 2 quarts beef broth
> ½ bell pepper, finely sliced
> 1 medium-sized onion, finely chopped
> 1 teaspoon chili powder

Blanch, peel, and seed tomatoes. Chop 3 of the seeded tomatoes and set aside. Crush the remaining tomatoes, add the peels, and simmer in the beef broth over a low flame. After 30 minutes, strain the tomato pulp and peels out of the broth. Add the bell pepper, onion, chili powder, and chopped tomatoes. Simmer until the albóndigas are ready.

Albóndigas:

> ½ *pound ground beef*
> ½ *pound ground pork*
> 1 *egg*
> 1 *teaspoon oregano*
> 3 *sprigs fresh mint, or 1 teaspoon*
> *powdered dried mint*
> ½ *onion, chopped*
> ⅓ *cup raw long-grain white rice*

Grind meat twice, or process until very fine. Whisk egg with herbs and onion then mix well into the meat. Soak rice in hot water for 15 minutes, then drain and add to the meat and herb mixture. Shape into little balls smaller than a walnut, and drop into the boiling broth. Cover tightly and cook for 30 minutes.

Serves 6–8.

Sopa de Albóndigas
de Polla

Soup with Chicken Balls Flavored with Mint

> 1 *chicken breast, poached (skinless*
> *and boneless)*
> ¼ *pound ham*
> 1 *slice French bread*
> *Sprigs of fresh mint (or parsley)*
> 2 *eggs*
> 2 *quarts double chicken broth (see*
> *p. 56)*

In a food processor or meat grinder, grind chicken, ham, and bread together. Add a few leaves of mint or parsley, finely minced. Stir in the eggs and mix well.

Shape into small balls, and drop into the hot broth. Simmer for about 20 minutes, then serve.

Serves 8.

Sopa de Albóndigas
de Pescado

Fish Ball Soup

The Soup:
> 1 *large halibut head and trimmings,*
> *or other firm white fish*
> 3 *quarts cold water*
> 1 *onion*
> 2 *cloves garlic*

1 teaspoon oregano
6 peppercorns
1 bay leaf
Salt to taste
Oil for frying
2 large potatoes, cubed
¼ cup tomato puree, or 1 medium-
   sized tomato, peeled, chopped, and
   seeded

Simmer together fish trimmings, water, onion, garlic, and herbs for about 30 minutes, until you have made a rich broth. Strain and set aside.

In a skillet, heat oil and cook potatoes and tomato puree (or tomatoes) for about 5 minutes. Add to the strained broth.

Fish Balls:
1½ pounds halibut or other mild,
   firm-fleshed fish
2 eggs, beaten
1 teaspoon oregano
Salt and pepper to taste
Slices of lemon and lime

Remove all bones and grind fish in meat grinder or food processor. Add eggs and spices and mix well. Roll into balls about 1½ inches in diameter and drop into boiling fish broth. Cover and simmer for about 30 minutes, then serve. Garnish with a slice of lemon or lime.

Serves 8.

Sopa de Bolita de Tortilla

Tortilla Ball Soup

6 *tortillas (they can be stale)*
½ *wedge (about ¼ pound)*
  Camembert cheese
1 *tablespoon butter*
1 *egg, lightly beaten*
Salt and pepper to taste
Pinch cayenne pepper
6 *cups double-rich chicken or beef*
  broth (see pp. 55–56)
½ *cup tomato puree (if using beef*
  broth)
Parmesan cheese

Soak tortillas in water, then grind in food processor or blender. Add cheese and blend again. Add butter, egg, salt, pepper, and a pinch of cayenne, and continue blending. Roll tortilla and cheese mixture into small balls, about the size of a cherry tomato.

Drop the balls into boiling-hot beef broth (to which you have added the tomato puree) or boiling-hot chicken broth, and poach balls for about 10 minutes.

Serve in individual soup bowls or in a tureen, with Parmesan cheese sprinkled on the top.

Serves 6.

Sopa de Pollo y Aguacate

Chicken Soup with Avocado

4 *tortillas (corn)*
Oil for frying
½ *onion, chopped*
1 *small (4-oz.) can chopped green chiles*
6 *cups chicken broth*
1½–2 *cups shredded cooked chicken*
1 *ripe tomato, peeled, seeded, and chopped*
1 *ripe avocado*
Fresh mint or fresh cilantro to garnish

Cut tortillas into ½-inch strips and fry in hot oil until crisp. Drain and set aside. In a large saucepan, heat a small amount of oil and add onions and green chiles. Sauté until just golden. Do not let onions brown. Add chicken broth and shredded chicken and simmer, covered, for about 15 minutes. Add chopped tomato and simmer a few minutes longer.

Peel and slice avocado.

To serve, ladle soup into individual soup bowls with a few tortilla strips in each bowl. Float avocado slice in each bowl, and garnish either with fresh mint sprigs or with a sprig of fresh cilantro.

Serves 6–8.

Sopa de Tortilla Yucatán

Tortilla Soup from Yucatán, Mexico

4 *tortillas (corn)*
Oil for frying
½ *onion, chopped*
1 *small (4-oz.) can chopped green chiles*
6 *cups chicken broth*
1½–2 *cups shredded cooked chicken*
1 *ripe tomato, peeled, seeded, and chopped*
2 *tablespoons lime juice*
Salt to taste
6–8 *thin slices of lime*

Cut tortillas into ½-inch strips and fry in hot oil until crisp. Drain and set aside. In a large saucepan, heat a small amount of oil and add onions and green chiles. Sauté until just golden. Do not let onions brown. Add the chicken broth and shredded chicken and cover. Simmer slowly for about 15 minutes. Add chopped tomato and simmer a few minutes longer. Stir in lime juice and add salt if needed.

To serve, ladle into individual soup bowls with a few tortilla strips in each bowl. Add a lime slice to float and serve.

Serves 6–8.

Caldo Tlalpeño

Chicken Soup from Tlalpán, Mexico

8 *cups chicken broth*
1 *whole chicken breast, skin on*
1 *tablespoon oil*
¼ *cup chopped onion*
1 *clove garlic, crushed*
1 *ripe tomato, peeled, seeded, and*
   finely chopped
1 *canned chipotle chile, drained*
6 *radishes, thinly sliced*
2 *scallions, thinly sliced*
1 *cup chick-peas (canned are fine)*
4 *ounces Muenster cheese, coarsely*
   grated
1 *ripe avocado, sliced*
Lime wedges

In a heavy saucepan, heat chicken broth until boiling. Reduce heat and add chicken breast. Simmer in broth until tender (about 20 minutes) and remove chicken from broth. When cool enough to handle, remove skin and bones, and shred chicken with your fingers or with the tines of 2 forks. You should have about 1–1½ cups of chicken.

In a skillet, heat oil and sauté onion and garlic until clear but not brown. Add tomato and stir over medium heat until most of the liquid has evaporated.

In a food processor or blender, puree chipotle chiles with about ½ cup of the chicken stock. Add chiles and tomato mixture to stock and stir over a low heat until flavors mix.

When ready to serve, divide chicken, radishes, scallions, chick-peas, and cheese evenly among 6 soup bowls.

Ladle chicken broth mixture into the bowls. Float a few slices of avocado in each bowl, and serve with a lime wedge on the side.

Serves 8.

Caldo Xochipili

Chicken Soup from Yucatán

> 6 *cups chicken stock*
> 1 *whole chicken breast, skin on*
> ¼ *cup vegetable or peanut oil*
> ¼ *pound spaghettini or vermicelli*
> 2 *serrano chiles*
> 1 *ripe avocado*
> *Salt and freshly ground pepper to taste*

In a large saucepan, place the chicken breast in the chicken stock and simmer, tightly covered, for about 30 minutes. Remove the chicken and, when cool enough to handle, skin, bone, and cut into bite-sized pieces.

While chilcken is cooking, heat the oil in a skillet. Break the spaghettini into 2-inch lengths and cook in the oil, stirring constantly, until pale-gold in color. Drain on paper towels.

Bring chicken stock back to a boil and add spaghettini, simmering until tender (about 7 minutes). Add the chicken. Chop the chiles and add them to the soup. Peel and seed the avocados and cut into 1-inch cubes. Add to the soup, with salt and pepper to taste, and serve.

Serves 6.

Sopa de Pollo con Elote

Chicken and Corn Soup

> 1 frying chicken, quartered
> 4 cups water
> 1 small onion
> 1 stalk celery, quartered
> 1 medium-sized carrot, quartered
> ¼ teaspoon peppercorns
> ½ teaspoon coriander seeds
> Salt to taste
> 6 ears fresh corn, or 2 packages frozen
> 2 medium-sized tomatoes, peeled,
> seeded, and chopped

Place chicken in saucepan with water, onion, celery, carrot, peppercorns, coriander, and salt. Cover and bring to a boil. Reduce the heat and simmer for 45 minutes. Remove chicken and set aside.

Strain the stock into another cooking pot.

Cut the kernels of corn off the cobs. Add kernels to the strained chicken stock and cook for 10 minutes (less if using frozen corn). Remove chicken from bones and cut into strips. Add chicken to stock. Stir in tomatoes and simmer for another 10 minutes.

Serves 6–8.

Caldo de Friars

Priests' Soup

2 tablespoons cooking oil or butter
3 shallots, sliced
3 green chiles, sliced (canned will
  do—use 1 small [3 oz.] can)
1 clove garlic, minced
Sprigs of parsley to taste
½ head cabbage, finely chopped
4 cups chicken broth, or water
1 tomato (optional)
Slices of lemon
3 jalapeño peppers, sliced (preferably
  fresh, but you can substitute 1 small
  [3 oz.] can)

Heat oil or butter in a heavy Dutch oven and cook the shallots until they are translucent. Add the chiles, garlic, and parsley and cook in the butter or oil. Add cabbage and either chicken stock or water and simmer until cabbage is tender. You may add a blanched tomato, peeled, seeded, and chopped, if you desire.

Serve with a slice of lemon on top, and hot chopped jalapeños in a small dish to pass.

Serves 4.

Sopa de Noche Buena

Soup for Christmas Eve

3½ quarts chicken broth
2 full chicken breasts, simmered in
  the broth
1 tomato, blanched, peeled,
  seeded, and chopped
2 scallions, chopped
1–2 green bell peppers, chopped
1–2 red bell peppers, chopped (fresh
  red bell is preferable, but if not
  available, you can use canned
  pimientos)
1 tortilla, finely ground
¼ cup sherry
1 cup whipping cream, whipped stiff

Poach chicken breasts in broth until tender (about 30 minutes). Remove from broth, and when cool enough to handle, skin, bone, and cut meat into small pieces.

Add the chopped tomato, scallions, and bell peppers to the broth and simmer for 30 minutes. Add ground tortilla to thicken. Return chicken to broth and simmer for just a few more minutes. (If using canned pimiento, add them with the cooked chicken.)

At serving time, add the sherry to the broth and heat well. Serve with a spoonful of whipped cream in each cup.

Makes about 12 servings.

Sopa de Quarto de Hora

15-Minute Soup

> ½ *pound clams, in the shell*
> 2 *tablespoons olive oil*
> 2 *ounces ham, diced*
> 1 *small onion, finely chopped*
> 2 *small tomatoes, blanched, peeled,*
>   *and seeded*
> ½ *teaspoon pasilla pepper or paprika*
> 4½ *cups boiling water*
> *Clam broth (optional)*
> ½ *pound raw shrimp, cleaned,*
>   *shelled, and deveined*
> ¼ *cup shelled peas*
> 2 *tablespoons raw rice*
> ½ *teaspoon salt*
> *Pinch black pepper*

Rinse clams and let sit in a bowl sprinkled with cornmeal to remove the grit. This can be done in the refrigerator overnight. Scrub the clams and cook in water to cover until they open. Remove 1 shell from each clam and set aside. If you wish, you may pass the cooking water through a gauze-lined strainer to remove all traces of sand, and set aside to use as clam broth.

Heat oil in a skillet and brown ham. Remove ham and sauté onion until translucent. Add tomatoes and simmer for 5 minutes. Remove from fire and add pasilla pepper or paprika. Pour in 4½ cups boiling water (preferably part clam broth). Add shrimp, peas, and drained, scalded rice, and season to taste. Simmer uncovered for 15 minutes. Just before serving, add ham and clams.

Serves 4–6.

Sopa de Media Hora

Half-Hour Soup

> 2 quarts chicken broth
> 6 zucchinis, sliced lengthwise, then
>   cut into ½-inch slices
> 1 large onion, chopped
> 6 carrots, sliced
> 2 ripe tomatoes, peeled, seeded, and
>   chopped
> Bay leaf
> Salt and freshly ground pepper
> 1 avocado, cut in slices

Heat chicken stock in a large stockpot. Add zucchini, onion, carrots, tomatoes, bay leaf, salt, and freshly ground pepper to stock. Cover and simmer until vegetables are tender, about 30 minutes.

Taste and correct seasoning. Remove the bay leaf.

Serve in individual bowls and float a slice of avocado in each bowl.

Serves 6–8.

Sopa de Flan

Soup with Custard Cubes

In France this would be called consommé royale, *but the little squares of custard dropped into a rich broth are known here by the Mexican name of flan and add a touch of elegance to a clear tomato-flavored consommé.*

> 1 medium-sized onion, finely chopped
> 4 tomatoes, peeled and seeded
> 6 cups double beef broth (see p. 55)
> 1 tablespoon minced parsley

Simmer the tomatoes and onion in a little broth until cooked through, then strain into the remainder of the broth and heat over a low flame until the flan is done.

The Flan:
> 3 eggs
> ½ cup milk
> Salt and pepper

Whisk the eggs, milk, and seasoning together and pour into a shallow buttered casserole. Place casserole in a pan of boiling water (a Mary's bath) and bake at 350° for 15 minutes. When custard is firm, dice. Drop 5 or 6 squares into each serving cup. Carefully pour the heated broth over them. Sprinkle with parsley.

Serves 6–8.

Sopa de Fideos

Vermicelli or Noodle Soup

> 2 tablespoons olive oil
> 2 ounces vermicelli or spaghettini,
>   uncooked
> 1 onion, chopped
> 1 clove garlic, chopped
> 4 ripe tomatoes, peeled, seeded, and
>   chopped
> 2 quarts beef broth (see recipe on
>   p. 55 or use a good-quality canned
>   beef broth—not bouillon)
> Salt and pepper
> 1 tablespoon chopped parsley
> ¼ cup dry sherry
> ¼ cup grated Parmesan cheese

Heat oil and sauté the noodles until golden-brown. Drain and set aside, but reserve the oil.

In food processor or blender, combine onion, garlic, and tomato, and puree. Place in pan with reserved oil and cook for about 5 minutes, stirring constantly. Place noodles, tomato puree, and stock in a large saucepan. Season to taste with salt and pepper, cover, and simmer gently until noodles are tender.

Add parsley and sherry right before serving.

Spoon into individual soup bowls and serve with Parmesan cheese on the side.

Serves 6.

Sopa de Frijoles

Pink Bean Soup

> 4 cups cooked pink beans, with
>   broth in which they were cooked
> 2 medium-sized tomatoes, peeled, or
>   2 cups canned tomatoes
> 1 clove garlic, peeled
> ¼ onion, chopped
> 3 tablespoons lard
> 2–3 cups chicken or beef broth
> Cubes of Muenster cheese
> 3 pasilla chiles, fried and crumbled
> Tortilla strips, fried crisp
> Sour cream, or crema (see p. 210)

Puree the beans with their broth in the jar of a blender. Remove beans and blend tomatoes, garlic, and onion until well pureed.

Melt the fat and cook the tomato mixture over a high flame for 5 minutes. Stir the bean puree into the tomato mixture and cook over a medium flame for about 10 minutes, stirring constantly. Add the broth and let soup cook for another 10 minutes. Taste and correct seasoning.

Have soup bowls ready with a few pieces of cheese in each bowl. Pour hot soup over them and garnish with chiles and tortilla strips. Pass a bowl of sour cream to add at the last minute.

Serves 6.

Sopa de Frijole Negro

Black Bean Soup

2 cups dried black beans
2 quarts water
1 large onion, finely chopped
3 cloves garlic, minced
1 ham hock, or ½ pound meaty
    pork bone
1 teaspoon oregano
½ cup tomato paste (or 2 medium-
    sized tomatoes, peeled and diced)
Salt to taste
Radishes, thinly sliced
Cabbage, finely shredded
Minced serrano chiles
Sour cream, or crema (see p. 210)
Slices of lime

Soak beans in cold water for 15 minutes. Rinse well and pick out any bad ones. In a soup pot, combine beans and water and bring to a boil. Reduce heat and simmer, covered, for 2 hours. Add onions, garlic, pork bone or ham hock, and oregano. Cover and simmer for 1½ hours until beans and pork are tender. Add tomato paste or tomatoes and simmer for another 10 minutes. Add salt to taste.

Serve soup, passing bowls of radishes, cabbage, chiles, sour cream or crema, and lime slices for garnish.

Serves 6.

Cold Gazpacho

This is an elegant cold soup that you can whip up in your blender in about 3 minutes, then chill and serve:

> 1 large clove garlic
> 1 bunch fresh parsley
> 2 scallions, cut in 1-inch pieces
> 1 (16-oz.) can crushed tomatoes
> ⅓ cup olive oil
> Juice 1 lemon
> Salt and pepper to taste
> 2 stalks celery or cucumber or both
> 1 green pepper
> Croutons
> Small bunch cilantro (*optional*)

In your blender jar, chop garlic, parsley, and scallions. Add the can of tomatoes and blend. Add olive oil slowly and continue to blend. Add lemon juice and salt and pepper to taste.

Pour into a pitcher or bowl and chill for a few hours in refrigerator until ready to serve. Serve with garnish of chopped celery, cucumbers, and green peppers, either added directly to the gazpacho or served in small ceramic bowls so that each guest may add his own. You may also pass a bowl of freshly toasted croutons and garnish with a sprig of cilantro.

Serves 6.

Sopa de Aguacate

Chilled Avocado Soup

A wonderful starter course for a sit-down dinner party or a light lunch.

> 2 large ripe avocados
> 1 cup whipping cream
> ½ cup milk
> 1 cup chicken broth
> 1 teaspoon lemon juice
> Salt and white pepper
> Tabasco sauce (optional)
> Sour cream
> Chives or cilantro to garnish

Peel avocados and remove seeds. Place in blender or food processor and add whipping cream, milk, and chicken broth. Blend until smooth. Add lemon juice, salt, and white pepper (and a dash of Tabasco), and blend again.

Chill and serve in individual bowls. Top with a spoonful of sour cream and garnish with chives or a sprig of cilantro.

Serves 6.

Menudo

Tripe Soup

In Mexico's capital, "Menudo para la cruda" is the cry that is heard on New Year's morning. The covered copper or earthenware stockpot with a soup of honeycomb tripe and hominy is considered the most salubrious antidote for too much champagne or tequila the night before. The first day of January, you'll find buckets of tripe soup on many a doorstep. It can be addicting.

>   5 pounds honeycomb tripe
>   1 tablespoon olive oil
>   2 cloves garlic
>   2 tomatoes, peeled, seeded, and
>   chopped
>   2 teaspoons coriander
>   1 teaspoon oregano
>   2 teaspoons chili powder
>   1 onion, chopped
>   Salt and pepper to taste
>   6 quarts water
>   1 veal knuckle, if possible
>   3 cups whole hominy
>   Fresh cilantro, green onions, and mint
>   as garnish

Wash the tripe, cut it in 2-inch squares, and simmer for a few minutes with olive oil and garlic in a Dutch oven or large pot. Add tomato, the herbs tied in a gauze bag, chili powder, onion, and salt and pepper to taste. Add veal knuckle and 4 quarts of water and cook over a low flame for 3 hours. If you don't have a veal knuckle, you may want to add 2 cups of diluted beef broth instead of water. Add 3 cups of whole hominy and cook 2 hours longer.

Offer bowls of chopped green onions, chopped mint leaves, and fresh sprigs of cilantro as a garnish.

Serves 12.

CHAPTER V

The Breads of Mexico

Before we concentrate on the tortilla, the mainstay of every Mexican *casita*, *hacienda*, or *rancho*, we want to tell you about the *bolillo*, the gift of Maximilian's French pastry chefs. If you cross the border and stop at a bakery on the Mexican side, you'll find an array of delicate puff paste creations. But the finest bequest of Maximilian's pastry chefs is the bolillo—a marvelous little French crusty roll—that is served all over Mexico and tastes better than it does in France.

Several years ago, the government mandated that the bolillo should be priced at twenty for one peso, so that any member of a poor family could survive . . . well, almost.

The bolillo can be served in many ways: split in half, filled with any cooked beef, pork, or chicken, a few thinly sliced onions, tomatoes, and pickled chile peppers, it is the definitive submarine sandwich. In Mexico, the truly authentic ingredient would be calves' brains. We mention it for the brave, but leave out the recipe!

77

Bolillos

Maximilian's French Rolls

> 2 *cups lukewarm water*
> 1 *package dry yeast*
> 1½ *teaspoons salt*
> 1½ *tablespoons sugar*
> 1½ *tablespoons lard*
> 5 *cups unbleached flour*
> 1 *tablespoon cornstarch*
> ⅓ *cup cold water*

Stir together warm water, yeast, salt, and sugar. Beat in lard with 2 cups of flour (much simpler with a processor), then beat in 2½ cups of flour to make a sticky dough. Flour a board with the remaining ½ cup of flour and turn out the dough. Knead for no longer than 5 minutes and then transfer the dough to a greased bowl. Let rise, covered, in a warm place until doubled in bulk (approximately 1½ hours). Punch down dough and divide into 13 balls. Roll each ball between your palms and pull into the shape of a football. Place on a greased baking sheet and with a sharp knife that has been dipped in cold water cut a slash on the top of each roll. Brush tops with cornstarch mixed with cold water and bake at 375° in a preheated oven for about 20 minutes until light golden-brown. Serve warm or reheat before serving.

Makes 13 rolls.

Tortillas

If you live in the West or Southwest, tortillas are readily available in most major supermarkets, and even fresher ones are sold in the small *mercados* of Hispanic neighborhoods. In the large supermarkets, you should be able to find fresh or frozen corn tortillas, diversely sized for tacos, enchiladas, and hors d'oeuvres. Flour tortillas are commonly offered in 6-, 8- and 12-inch diameters, and even larger ones can be found that are perfect for deluxe burritos.

If the Mexican food craze has not yet hit your hometown, and your local grocery chain does not stock tortillas, you can make them from scratch using the masa harina that is marketed and distributed by Quaker Oats and available in most parts of the country. But before you take on this task—which definitely shifts your adventure in Mexican cooking away from the "easy to prepare" realm—try talking to your local store manager and letting him know that he just might find a market for these wonderful and versatile edibles.

Failing the "squeaky wheel" approach, you can enjoy the fruits of your own labors with the recipes on the following pages.

Tortillas de Maíz

Corn Tortillas

Far from the city, a woman on the rancho used to make her tortillas in the following manner:

From masa (a mixture of dried corn cooked in a lime solution until the husks can be rubbed off) that is ground while still moist, she would make a small ball, about the size of an egg, and pat it between her two palms until a flat round pancake was formed. This was then cooked on a griddle—in Mexico, a comal—until done on both sides, but not browned.

Today, she would probably use a tortilla press. Lacking a tortilla press, the tortilla can also be pressed between layers of wax paper with a rolling pin.

Since you probably do not wish to grind your own masa, use the masa harina corn flour that is packed and shipped out of Chicago, and simply follow directions on the package.

If you have a gas flame, the process of heating a tortilla is simple. Don't burn your fingers—use tongs. Pass the tortilla over the flame, turning it constantly to heat it through. Then wrap in foil or a heavy napkin and keep covered until serving time.

Without a gas flame, use an ungreased griddle and turn the tortilla constantly. Stack and cover and keep warm in the oven.

To heat tortillas for a crowd, use an open rack in the oven and let them all heat, separated, for 7 minutes. Then stack them together and wrap in foil or a heavy napkin.

In a microwave, make 2 stacks of 6 tortillas each, and heat.

Note: If tortillas seem dry or brittle, before heating simply dampen them with a few drops of water and rub the moisture in with your palm. They will be as good as new!

Tortillas de Harina

Flour Tortillas

Introduced after wheat flour was brought into the Mexican state of Sonora, white-flour tortillas come in all sizes. On the ranchos, the little balls would be patted first to the size of the palm of one hand, then larger and thinner to the size from fingertip to wrist, and finally from wrist to elbow in diameter. You can buy flour tortillas made in 7-, 12-, and 14-inch circles. The larger 14-inch flour tortillas are most often used for burritos.

> 1 *pound sifted all-purpose flour*
> ½ *cup lard or other shortening*
> 1 *cup barely warm water*
> 2 *teaspoons salt*

If using a processor, you may need to divide the flour and lard into 2 batches. Whirl until well blended. Add water and salt and blend until it forms a ball. Combine both batches, and set aside for several hours. Do not refrigerate.

If mixing by hand, work the lard into the flour with your fingers. Dissolve the salt into water and add it to the flour mixture. Knead the dough for about 3 minutes. Set aside, covered, for at least 2 hours. Do not refrigerate.

Heat your griddle to medium. Knead the dough again for 1–2 minutes, then take a piece of the dough and roll it into a ball about 2 inches in diameter. Press the ball evenly onto a floured board. With a rolling pin, roll the ball of dough into a 7-inch circle, paper-thin. With each press, turn the dough around to keep it circular.

Place the dough on the ungreased griddle. It should sizzle as the dough touches it. Leave it for 20 seconds. If it puffs up, flatten it back on the griddle with the back of a spatula. Turn the tortilla over and cook it for a slightly shorter time on the other side. When cooked, place each one in a plastic bag, one atop the other. They should be thin and flexible. Make them in advance and warm them slightly on the griddle just prior to using.

Pan de Muerto

Bread of the Dead

The pan de muerto is traditionally served on November 2, All Saints' Day, when the Mexican people visit the graves of their family members to pay their respects. The bread is decorated with "bones" made of dough and shaped into a cross before baking. Pan de muerto is wonderful with coffee or Mexican chocolate.

½ cup milk
¼ cup sugar
1 teaspoon salt
¼ cup shortening, or part shortening/
    part butter
1 egg, plus an extra yolk, beaten
1 package yeast
2¾ cups sifted flour

Bring milk just to a boil. Remove from burner, stir in sugar, salt, and shortening. Add eggs and yeast and beat well. Add flour to liquid and mix to form a fairly stiff dough. Turn the dough onto a floured board and knead until dough is smooth. Cover with a damp cloth and let rest on the board for 30 minutes.

Cut the dough into 3 equal-sized pieces and roll each piece into a 12-inch rope. Remember to cut off enough dough to make the crossbones.

Make a braid of the 3 ropes and press the ends together to seal them. Place the braid on a lightly greased cookie sheet that has been dusted with flour. To be authentic, make 2 small "bone" shapes from the dough you have set aside. Lay them together in a cross, and decorate the top of the loaf. Cover with a damp cloth and let the dough rise in a protected warm place for about 1½ hours, until doubled in bulk. Brush with sweet butter and bake in a 375° preheated oven for 30 minutes.

Cool, and frost if desired.

Frosting:
Place ¼ cup boiling water in a small mixing bowl and sift in powdered sugar until the mixture reaches frosting consistency. Spread lightly on the bread and serve.

Makes 1 loaf.

Pan de Maíz

Mexican Corn Bread

> 1 *cup cornmeal*
> 1 *cup all-purpose flour*
> 1 *tablespoon baking powder*
> 1 *teaspoon salt*
> 1 *egg*
> 1 *cup milk*
> 4 *ears corn, or 1 cup cream-style corn*
> ¼ *cup chopped onion*
> 2 *tablespoons chopped green chiles*
> 2 *tablespoons chopped pimiento*
> ¼ *cup butter*
> ½ *cup shredded cheddar cheese*

Combine dry ingredients in a bowl and mix well. Beat egg and milk together. Add corn cut from the cob or from the can. Mix well. In skillet sauté onion, chiles, and pimiento in butter until onion is tender. Add milk mixture, onion mixture, and cheese to dry ingredients. Stir until just mixed. Pour into well-buttered 8-inch square pan. Bake in preheated 400° oven for 35 minutes.

Makes 9 2⅔-inch squares or stuffing for a chicken or turkey.

Rosca de Reyes

Twelfth Night Christmas Bread

On Twelfth Night, this slightly sweetened bread ring is served with a thimble or a bean hidden inside the dough. The person who gets the secret treasure must give a party on el Dia de la Candelaría, February 2, the Day of the Candle Mass.

> 2 *packages yeast*
> 2 *tablespoons lukewarm water*
> ⅔ *cup milk, scalded*
> ⅓ *cup sugar*
> 1½ *teaspoons salt*
> 3 *eggs, beaten to a lemon-yellow*
> ⅓ *cup soft butter*
> 4 *cups sifted flour*
> 2 *cups currants, soaked in brandy*

Soften yeast in water. In a separate bowl blend scalded milk, sugar, and salt. When cooled, add softened yeast, beaten eggs, butter, and half the flour. Beat with a wooden spoon until blended. Add remaining flour and currants. Mix until dough is moderately stiff. Knead lightly on a floured board to smooth out dough.

Divide the dough in half and roll each half into a long rope shape, about 20 inches in length. Form each rope into a circle and place on a greased cookie sheet. Brush with melted butter and let rise in slightly warm place until the dough doubles in bulk—about 1 hour. Don't forget to hide the bean in the dough! Bake in a 375° oven for 25–30 minutes. Let cool before slicing.

To decorate, make a thin icing of sifted powdered sugar mixed with enough milk to give it a spreading consistency. Spread over loaf and decorate with chopped walnuts.

Makes 2 rings.

Empanadas and Empanaditas

Turnovers

The Russians call them piroshki; the English call them meat pies, and usually make them larger. These little turnovers can be served with cocktails or with a sweet filling for dessert. For appetizers, they should be made very small, no bigger around than the rim of a whiskey glass.

The Dough:

> 1 teaspoon salt
> 2 cups flour
> 2 teaspoons baking powder
> ⅔ cup lard
> Ice water to blend

Sift the salt, flour, and baking powder together. Then mix in the lard as you would for a pastry dough, using 2 knives, 2 fingers, or a food processor. Add ice water, drop by drop, if needed to hold together. Roll into a ball, cover, and chill for several hours. Then divide into balls (12 for larger empanadas, 24 for appetizer size) and roll into rounds, about ⅛-inch thick. Place a spoonful of filling on half of each round, then fold over and seal, pressing the edges with dampened fingers.

Either fry the empanadas in hot oil until golden-brown and drain on paper towels, or bake for 15–20 minutes in a 400° oven.

Suggested Fillings for Empanadas:
Grated cheddar cheese with diced green chiles
Shredded chicken, Monterey Jack cheese, diced green chiles, and sautéed onions
Any leftover meats, mixed with your favorite salsa
Creamed chicken with chives
Minced crabmeat or shrimp, with cooked tomato, onion, and pimiento
Chopped smoked salmon, sour cream, and chopped cucumbers
Machaca, picadillo, or ropa vieja (see Index)

Suggested Fillings for Empanadas Dulces (Dessert Turnovers):
Any jam or preserve
Guava or quince paste
Mincemeat
Coconut mixed with raisins, pineapple, and almonds
Any pie filling
Sprinkle empanadas dulces with granulated sugar just before baking

CHAPTER VI

Comidas Típicas
Traditional Mexican Dishes

**Tortilla Dishes
(Including Tacos, Tostadas,
Taquitos, Quesadillas,
Enchiladas, Burritos,
Gorditas, and Tamales)**

**Suggested Meat Fillings
for Comidas Típicas**

Tortilla Dishes

What can we do with a tortilla?

Make a taco. Crisp-fry it, fold it carefully, and stuff it with varying combinations of meat, chicken, crab, cheese, lettuce, and vegetables. Then add a piquant sauce.

Make a soft taco. Simply warm it and fill with any leftovers you have on hand. Add salsa and sour cream.

Stack a dozen tortillas and place your fillings and sauces between each layer. Then cut the whole thing like a cake.

Tear it up and make chilequiles with eggs for breakfast, with chicken and cheese for brunch.

Fold it in half over a creamy cheese with slices of green chiles and have a quesadilla.

Cut it in strips and fry, then drop sizzling into a rich, flavorful broth.

And, of course, the whole enchilada!

Recipes for all to follow.

Tacos

Tacos are the Mexican equivalent to the American sandwich, and like a sandwich can be as simple or complex as time and taste will allow. A taco may be simply a heated tortilla folded over a bit of filling or a wonderful creation such as our taco fantasía de Carlota. The tortillas can be warmed to soften and folded over the filling; they may be deep-fried into a taco shell and then filled with various fillings; they may be softened, filled, and folded, and then deep-fried.

FILLINGS: Shredded chicken, shredded beef, shredded pork, refried beans, strips of steak, steak and chorizo, beef with potatoes, or any combination that sounds good.

GARNISHES: Sour cream, guacamole, avocado slices, grated cheese, shredded lettuce, chopped tomatoes, black olives, chopped scallions, red onion slices, and so on. (One of my favorite restaurants in Los Angeles serves chicken tacos topped with Caesar salad—not authentic, but certainly delicious!)

SAUCES: Any sauce that tastes delicious on another dish will taste as good on a taco—simple salsa cruda, tomatillo sauce, mole, salsa picante, and the like. The salsa cruda, made with chopped tomatoes and spices (see page 29), is the most commonly served.

TACOS—CRISP: To make a taco shell, heat about ¼ of an inch of vegetable oil (or lard) in a skillet. Dip a corn tortilla in the hot oil and fry quickly to soften. With tongs, fold the tortilla in half and continue to fry—folded—until both sides are crisp and golden. Drain on paper towels and repeat until you have prepared as many taco shells as you need. If you keep them in a warm oven on a dish lined with paper towels, they will stay warm and continue to drain.

To fill the taco shells, open gently, just wide enough to place a spoonful or two of your favorite filling—shredded chicken, shredded or ground beef, pork, and so on—in the center. Top the filling with various garnishes, such as shredded iceberg lettuce, chopped tomatoes, chopped scallions, and grated cheese.

TACOS—FRIED: You can also cook your tacos with the filling inside. Heat each tortilla on your open gas flame or griddle just until soft enough to fold, or wrap a stack of tortillas in foil and place them in a 350° oven until they have softened. Place a small amount of filling on each warmed tortilla and fold in half. Secure each taco with a toothpick and fry a few at a time in a skillet of hot oil, turning to fry both sides. Drain on paper towels and serve with garnishes passed in individual bowls. Remember to remove the toothpicks before you serve your tacos!

Taco Fantasía de Carlota

Empress Taco

The star-crossed, ill-fated empress of Mexico, who adored her adopted country's spicy foods, might have chosen this as her favorite dish.

> 1 *filet mignon for each serving, or*
> 1 *chateaubriand for 6*
> Beurre manié (*butter and flour rolled*
> *into almond-sized balls*)
> 2 *cloves garlic, minced*
> 2 *sprigs parsley, minced*
> 1 *cup guacamole (see p. 43)*
> 1 *cup salsa fresca (see p. 29)*
> 3 *cups refried beans (see p. 159)*

Broil the steaks your way. When you turn them for the final browning, dot the tops with *beurre manié*, garlic, and parsley.

Serve the steak or sliced chateaubriand surrounded by a bouquet of 3 tablespoons of guacamole, 3 tablespoons of salsa fresca, and a serving of refried beans. Two warmed tortillas come folded on the side, so that each person can make his own taco.

Any steak from flank to sirloin tip will do just as well, but the above steaks are the ultimate fantasy.

Serves 6.

Tostadas

Tostadas are tortillas—corn or flour—fried crisp and covered with different layers of fillings, sauces, and garnishes. Made on a large flour tortilla, a tostada can be an entire meal, and makes a beautiful luncheon dish. Made on a small flour or corn tortilla, with just beans and salad garnishes, a tostada is a perfect side dish to a main entree.

Like the taco, tostadas are made with many combinations of fillings and garnishes—shredded chicken, beef or pork, refried beans, avocado or guacamole, sour cream, lettuce, tomatoes, grated cheese, onions, olives, radishes—whatever combinations appeal to your eye and palate.

To assemble, begin with a crisp tortilla (one that has been fried on both sides in hot oil), on which you place a layer of refried beans and then meat. Follow this with layers of shredded lettuce, tomato, and grated cheese. Top with sour cream, avocado, or guacamole. Finally, the garnishes—olives, radishes, scallions, whatever you like. Pass a bowl of salsa cruda.

Note: You may fry the tortillas the day before and crisp them in the oven just before serving. If you assemble all your ingredients in advance, do not put them together on the tortilla until the last minute so that your tostada does not get soggy.

TORTILLA CONCHAS: Here's an ingenious method for making a tortilla concha—an edible fluted bowl. Use your concha as you would a tortilla prepared for a tostada—fill it with beans, meat, shredded lettuce, grated cheese, and garnishes. It makes a prettier presentation and for a special meal would be worth the extra effort.

For each concha, place a warmed (pliable) tortilla, either flour or corn, under the bottom of an empty soup can. Take one piece of string and place it along the bottom of the tortilla, bringing it up the sides and tying it at the top. Repeat with a second piece of string, bringing it up the can on opposite sides, forming an "X" at the top of the can. Tie the second piece of string, and the tortilla should be secured in shape around the soup can. Using tongs, immerse can and tortilla into a deep pan of hot oil and deep-fry until the tortilla is crisp. Drain and cool slightly before removing string.

Repeat for as many tortilla conchas as you have guests to serve. You can reheat the conchas in a warm oven for a few minutes before serving.

Taquitos
(Little Rolled Tacos)

Taquitos (little rolled tacos) are corn tortillas rolled with a filling and fried. Taquitos can be filled with shredded beef, chicken, steak and chorizo, or seasoned ground beef. Served with guacamole sauce, they make a wonderful appetizer or any-time-of-the-day snack. For Clementina, who has cooked for my children for years, the idea of a recipe for taquitos would be absurd. She simply opens the refrigerator and uses whatever leftovers are available, shreds them, seasons them, and rolls them into taquitos, which are usually devoured right out of the pan. (P. H.)

Taquitos

Little Rolled Tacos

> 12 corn tortillas
> 1–1¼ cups filling—shredded meat,
> chicken, or ground beef
> Oil for frying
> Guacamole sauce (see p. 31)

Wrap tortillas in foil and heat in the oven just until they are soft and pliable (about 15 minutes). For each taquito, place a generous tablespoon of filling in a narrow strip along one end of each tortilla. Roll up tightly, fastening the taquito with a toothpick. In about 1 inch of hot oil, fry several taquitos at a time until they are crisp and golden. Drain on paper towels and serve with guacamole sauce.

Serves 6.

Note: Taquitos can be frozen and reheated in a medium-hot oven (350°–400°) for 20 minutes or until heated through.

Quesadillas

A basic quesadilla is a flour tortilla folded over on itself with cheese melted in the center. But take that basic idea, add green chiles, chorizo, cooked shredded chicken, green onions, and fresh tomatoes, then garnish with guacamole (see p. 43), sour cream, salsa, and black olives . . . and you can see that a quesadilla is a perfect appetizer-main course-breakfast-snack-side-dish—and always delicious.

Using flour tortillas, grate longhorn cheddar, or Monterey Jack cheese (or a combination of both) onto half of the tortilla. Add a few strips of green chile (canned poblano is fine), and fold the empty half of the tortilla over the filled half to form a half-moon.

Place the filled tortilla on a greased baking sheet to bake in a 400° oven until slightly browned and the cheese is melted; or, for a more flavorful quesadilla, sauté quickly on both sides in sweet butter. You can also make a perfect quesadilla on the flat side of a waffle iron—simply cook until the cheese filling is melted!

If serving as an appetizer, cut into wedges and arrange in a fan shape on a serving plate, decorated with tomato slices and olives on the side. Serve with dollops of sour cream, guacamole, and pass a fresh salsa.

Vary your fillings according to your own taste—use your imagination!

Enchiladas

Enchiladas are made from corn tortillas that have been softened in hot lard or cooking oil, dipped in sauce, filled with a precooked filling, then rolled and baked in a baking dish. Cooks who pride themselves on a neat kitchen generally fry the tortillas first, then dip them in sauce before rolling. Cooks who are less concerned with cleanup usually dip them in sauce, then fry them. They are delicious either way, filled with beef, cheese, chicken, or pork and dipped in a classic salsa roja (red sauce, see p. 34). But enchiladas can be as creative as the cook preparing them— fill them with pork and dip them in tomatillo sauce (see p. 36), or stuff them with crabmeat and cover them in green or red sauce. Fill them with chicken, and cover them with any sauce—red, green, creamy, spicy. Garnish with sliced olives, with radish roses, with chopped scallions, with dollops of sour cream, with guacamole (see p. 43)—any and all of these wonderful additions give this classic main dish its color and appeal when you serve it.

Enchiladas

A simple recipe for beef or chicken enchiladas, using canned sauce:

> ½ cup cooking oil
> 12 corn tortillas
> 1 (19-oz.) can enchilada sauce
>   or red chile sauce
> 2 cups shredded cooked chicken or
>   beef (to make plain cheese
>   enchiladas, substitute 1 pound of
>   shredded mild cheddar for the meat
>   or chicken)
> 1 pound cheese (Monterey Jack or
>   cheddar or both)
> 1 medium-sized onion, finely chopped

In a skillet, heat oil for frying and dip each tortilla in, frying quickly on each side just until soft. In another skillet, or a shallow saucepan, heat enchilada sauce until warm. Dip the fried tortilla in the red chile or enchilada sauce. Place about 2 tablespoons of shredded meat or chicken on the dipped tortilla, then add a sprinkling of the cheese, grated, and some of the chopped onion. Roll the tortilla around the meat mixture and place, seam side down, in a buttered baking dish. Repeat with each tortilla until you have completed all 12.

Pour remaining sauce on top and bake in a 350° oven for about 15 minutes, or until hot and bubbly. Grate additional cheese on top and let it melt over the enchiladas.

Garnish the dish with chopped scallions, dollops of sour cream, olives, and radishes.

Serves 6.

Enchiladas Verdes con Pollo

Green Chicken Enchiladas

> 1 *chicken, about 3½ pounds*
> 1 *medium-sized onion, chopped*
> 2 *stalks celery, chopped*
> 2 *carrots, chopped*
> 1 *small turnip, chopped*
> 1 *small parsnip, chopped*
> 4 *sprigs parsley*
> 1 *clove garlic*
> *Salt and pepper to taste*
> *Oil for frying*
> 12 *corn tortillas*
> 2 *cups tomatillo sauce (see page 36)*
> 6 *ounces Monterey Jack cheese,*
> *shredded*
> 2 *cups sour cream*
> *Black olives and pimientos*

Place chicken in a large pot with onions, celery, carrots, turnip, parsnip, parsley, garlic, pepper, and salt. Add water to cover and heat to boiling. Reduce heat and simmer, uncovered, for about 1 hour. Remove chicken and let cool. When cool enough to handle, remove skin and bones, and shred chicken either with fingers or the tines of a fork.

Heat oil in a heavy skillet and fry tortillas a few at a time until softened, about 10–15 seconds. Remove with tongs and drain on paper towels. Repeat with remaining tortillas.

Dip tortillas, one at a time, in tomatillo sauce. Place about ¼ cup chicken in center of tortilla and add cheese. Roll up and place seam side down in a greased shallow baking pan. Repeat with remaining tortillas.

Spoon remaining tomatillo sauce over enchiladas. Bake, covered with foil, for about 10 minutes at 350°. Uncover and bake until enchiladas are heated through— about 10 minutes.

Remove from oven and add grated cheese on the top. Spoon sour cream over enchiladas and serve.

Garnish with black olives and pimientos for color.

Serves 6.

Enchiladas Verdes con Puerco

Green Enchiladas with Pork Filling

Canned green tomatillos and canned green chiles form the base of these delectable enchiladas.

The Sauce:

    4 *tablespoons oil or butter for frying*
    2 *green onions, minced*
    1 *(4-oz.) can green chiles, chopped*
    2 *(10-oz.) cans tomatillos*
    1 *teaspoon oregano*
    1 *garlic clove, mashed*
    4 *tablespoons flour*
1½ *cups chicken broth*
1½ *cups milk or half and half*

Fry the onion until translucent. Add chiles and sauté lightly. Drain and rinse tomatillos, then add along with oregano and garlic. Mash down with a fork and cook until heated through. Sprinkle flour over the top and stir over low heat for 2–3 minutes. Add chicken broth and milk. Stir well until blended, then simmer until well thickened, about 20 minutes. Stir from time to time to keep from scorching.

The Filling:

> 2 pounds lean pork, cut into ½-inch cubes
> 1 clove garlic
> 1 onion, minced
> 1 tomato, chopped
> Salt and pepper

> 12 tortillas
> Oil for frying

In a heavy pot or Dutch oven, place the meat and garlic with just enough water to cover. Cover the pot and cook until meat is tender (about 45 minutes). Remove the lid and allow the meat to cook until brown and a little crusty. Add the onion, tomato, and seasonings, and cook for 7 minutes longer. Add about ½ cup of the green sauce to the meat mixture and let stand while preparing the tortillas.

Fry the tortillas lightly, just enough to make them limp, and then dip into the sauce. Add the meat stuffing with a tablespoon of the sauce, then roll and place seam side down in a greased baking dish.

These enchiladas may be made ahead of time, and heated later in the oven at 500°. Pour the sauce over them just before heating. Save some of the heated sauce and pass when serving.

Makes 12 enchiladas.

Enchiladas Suizas

Swiss Enchiladas

Because at one time Mexico thought of Switzerland as a dairy country, enchiladas that use cream in the sauce are known as enchiladas Suizas. For those who don't trust Mexican food, these are a good starter, because they are mild and muy delicioso.

        1 medium-sized onion, chopped
    Oil for frying
        1 small (4-oz.) can green chiles, diced
        2 cups tomatillos, drained and rinsed
        2 tablespoons flour
     1½ cups chicken broth
        2 cups cooked chicken
        1 cup sweet cream, warmed
    Salt to taste
       12 tortillas
      ½ pound Monterey Jack cheese,
            grated

Fry the onion in hot oil until translucent. Add diced green chiles and sauté with the onions until soft. In a blender jar, puree the tomatillos, and add to the chiles and onions and stir. Sprinkle in the flour and stir over low heat for 2–3 minutes. Add chicken broth and simmer until sauce is quite thick. Take half the tomatillo sauce and add it to the chicken. Mix the remaining half of the sauce with the warmed cream.

Fry each tortilla in an inch of oil until soft and pliable. Dip each tortilla in the cream and tomatillo mixture. Arrange in a baking dish, place a few tablespoons of chicken and some cheese in the tortilla, and roll, placing seam side down in the baking dish. Just before baking, pour the creamy sauce over the entire dish and top with remaining cheese. Add salt to taste. Heat through (about 30 minutes at 350°) and serve.

Makes 12 enchiladas.

Crabmeat Enchiladas with Salsa Verde

This is a pure California variation on the enchilada, but very tasty!

> ½ cup cooking oil
> 12 corn tortillas
> 2 cups tomatillo sauce (see p. 36)
> 2 cups crabmeat
> 1 pound Monterey Jack cheese, grated
> 4 scallions, chopped
> Sour cream

In a skillet, heat oil and dip each tortilla, frying quickly on each side until just limp. In another skillet, warm the tomatillo sauce. Dip the fried tortilla in tomatillo sauce. Place crabmeat and grated Monterey Jack cheese on the tortilla. Sprinkle with chopped scallions and roll. Place in a buttered baking dish, seam side down, until you have completed all 12.

Pour remaining tomatillo sauce on top, grate cheese over sauce, and bake in a 300° oven until hot and bubbly.

Garnish with scallions and large dollops of sour cream.

Makes 1 dozen.

Enchiladas de Pollo con Mole

Chicken Enchiladas with Mole Sauce

For the sauce, use the recipe for mole poblano on page 40, or the simplified version, mole sencillo, on page 39.

> 2 double chicken breasts, or 1 whole
>   fryer, cut up
> ½ cup cooking sherry (optional)
> Oil for frying
> ½ small onion, chopped
> 2 tablespoons oregano
> 2 cloves garlic, minced
> ½ teaspoon cumin
> 1 large tomato, peeled, seeded, and
>   chopped
> 12 tortillas
> ¾ pound Monterey Jack cheese, grated

Poach the chicken breasts or chicken in salted water with sherry. Simmer over a low flame for 25 minutes. Remove from heat and cool. When cool enough to handle, remove chicken from bones and pull apart into bite-sized pieces. Heat 1 tablespoon of oil in a medium-sized skillet. Add onion and stir until translucent. Add oregano, garlic, and cumin, and stir over heat. Add tomato, and cook until soft. Add chicken pieces and mix well.

Fry the tortillas one at a time in oil until just softened but not browned or crisp. Drain on paper towels. Dip into warmed mole sauce and place on a flat plate. Put chicken mixture in a line down center of tortilla and sprinkle with cheese. Roll tortilla around filling and place seam side down in a shallow baking dish, preferably glass or earthenware. When all tortillas are filled and rolled, top with remaining mole sauce and sprinkle with remaining cheese.

Bake at 350° until cheese is melted and enchiladas are heated through (about 25 minutes).

If enchiladas are prepared the day before, do not pour the sauce over them until baking time.

Makes 12 enchiladas.

Enchiladas Inez

Inez's Enchiladas

From the kitchen of Inez Juarez comes this recipe for easy-to-make enchiladas . . . easy, because they are stacked and layered instead of rolled.

Red Sauce for Enchiladas:
>   3 *tablespoons oil*
>   2 *tablespoons flour*
>   1 *clove garlic, mashed*
>   2 *cups tomato puree*
>   1 *cup hot beef stock*
>   2 *tablespoons (or more) chili powder*
>   *Pinch cumin*
>   1 *small (3-oz.) can pitted olives*

Brown flour in oil. Add garlic and tomato puree and stir. In a separate pot, heat the beef stock and add chili powder. When dissolved, stir into the tomato sauce mixture. Season with cumin, cover, and simmer for 10 minutes. Keep warm until filling is ready.

Enchilada Filling:

    3 chorizos
    ½ pound ground round
    2 green onions, minced
    Oil or lard for frying
    12 tortillas
    ¾ pound Monterey Jack or Muenster
       cheese

Remove chorizos from their casings and fry without adding fat, but do not brown. Add ground round and stir until all the meat is well browned. Add the onions and cook for 5 minutes, adding a bit of oil if required.

Dip each tortilla into the hot sauce, then fry lightly in hot oil or lard. Cover the bottom of a casserole with the fried tortillas (2 or 3), then add a layer of the meat and chorizo mixture. Break up the cheese and sprinkle the bits over the entire layer. Place 2 or 3 tortillas over the filling and add another layer of meat and cheese. Continue layering with the final topping of tortillas. Then pour remaining sauce over the dish and garnish with sliced olives.

This can be made in advance and heated in a medium (350°) oven for about 30 minutes.

Serves 6.

Enchiladas de Margarita

Margaret's Enchiladas

Margarita called these "enchiladas exquisitos," because they were very special.

The Filling:

>1 *pound ground beef, chuck or round*
>2 *tablespoons oil or lard*
>1 *chorizo (see p. 116)*
>3 *green onions, minced*
>2 *tomatoes, peeled, seeded, and
>   chopped*
>Pinch cumin
>Pinch oregano

The Sauce:

>1 *onion, minced*
>1 *garlic clove, mashed*
>2 *tablespoons cooking oil*
>2 *tablespoons flour*
>1 *large (28-oz.) can red enchilada sauce,
>   or 3 cups salsa roja (see p. 34)*

>12 *tortillas*
>Oil for frying
>1 *cup sour cream*
>1 *cup chopped walnuts*

Sauté the ground beef in hot oil with the chorizo, which has been removed from its casing and crumbled. When well browned, add the onions and tomatoes, and stir. Simmer for 20 minutes uncovered. Add the cumin and oregano and stir well. Keep warm while you prepare the tortillas.

If you are using the canned enchilada sauce, simmer the onion and garlic in a little oil, sprinkle with flour, and stir until flour is well blended. Then add the canned sauce and stir until heated through.

Dip each tortilla in the sauce, then fry lightly until pliable. Fill with the meat mixture, roll, and place seam side down in a baking dish. Pour half the sauce over the enchiladas and bake for 20 minutes in a 350° oven. Cover with sour cream and sprinkle with chopped walnuts and heat for 5 minutes more.

Makes 12 enchiladas.

Burritos

Burritos are warmed flour tortillas wrapped around a beef or bean-and-beef filling, and eaten sandwich-style or served with sauce.

To make a burrito, warm a flour tortilla on a hot griddle or over a gas flame until soft but not dry. Place filling (about ¼–½ cup) in the center of the warmed tortilla and fold the sides over the filling to meet at the center. Fold the bottom of the tortilla up over the filling and roll so that the filling is completely enclosed. Eat like a sandwich or serve on a platter covered with a red enchilada sauce.

FILLINGS: Typically, burritos are filled with refried beans and grated cheese (Monterey Jack or cheddar or combination), with shredded beef and beans, with beef and chorizo and beans, or even a favorite chile con carne recipe. You may want to add avocado or shredded lettuce or sour cream before folding it up, but be sure you assemble at the last minute before serving. Burritos can get soggy if they are not served right away.

FRIED BURRITOS, OR CHIMICHANGAS: Particularly delicious if you are working with good flaky flour tortillas, a chimichanga is a deep-fried burrito. Eliminate the lettuce and add sour cream as a final garnish after frying. Delicious!

Chilorio

Pork Filling for Burritos

White flour tortillas can be found 7, 12, or 14 inches in diameter. It is usually the larger tortillas that are rolled up and filled with pork and refried beans to make a burrito.

>   2 *pounds pork (shoulder or butt)*
>   5 *ancho chiles (dried)*
>   4 *cloves garlic*
>   ¼ *teaspoon oregano*
>   ⅛ *teaspoon cumin*
>   ⅓ *cup liquid—water mixed with either vinegar or white wine*

Cut the pork into 1-inch squares. Cover with water and cook for 45 minutes, or until water has evaporated and the meat has barely browned. Remove meat from the pan and shred it with the tines of 2 forks. Save the fat that has been rendered.

Slit the chiles and remove seeds and veins. Cover with hot water and soak for 15 minutes. In a blender, mix chiles, garlic, herbs, and diluted vinegar or wine until smooth and resembling a thick paste.

Add enough lard to the pork drippings to make ¼ cup. Add meat and sauce and mix well. Simmer over a low flame for 20 minutes, until meat is well seasoned.

Place 4 or 5 tablespoons of filling in the center of a 14-inch tortilla that has been softened in a low oven. If using a smaller tortilla, place 2 tablespoons of filling. Fold the ends like an envelope. Turn seam side down on a plate and serve with guacamole (see p. 43) and sour cream on the side.

For other fillings, see pp. 116–122.

Enough for 8–10 large burritos.

Chimichangas

Deep-Fried Burritos

> 1 *large onion, finely chopped*
> 3 *cloves garlic, blanched and*
>   *mashed*
> *Oil or lard*
>   2 *cups cooked pinto or pink beans,*
>   *or 1 cup tomato puree*
>   2 *jalapeño chiles, seeded and*
>   *minced*
>   2 *cups cooked ground beef, cooked*
>   *shredded beef, or cooked*
>   *shredded pork*
>   ½ *teaspoon cumin*
> *Salt to taste*
> *8–10 flour tortillas (12")*
> *Guacamole (see p. 43)*
> *Sour cream or crema (see p. 210)*

Sauté onion and garlic in oil or lard in a heavy frying pan until softened. Drain beans, reserving liquid, and add to the skillet. Mash the beans with onions and garlic, adding some liquid to make a slightly moist mixture. (If you are not using beans, substitute 1 cup of tomato puree.) Continue to heat, adding chiles, meat, cumin, and salt to taste. When the mixture is hot, put 2 tablespoons in the middle of a tortilla, fold like an envelope, and secure with a toothpick. Fry the stuffed tortilla in 1 inch of hot oil until browned on both sides. Drain on paper towels and serve hot with guacamole and sour cream.

If these are made ahead of time, they can be reheated in foil in a 350° oven for 12–15 minutes. If taken from the freezer, allow 25 minutes to heat.

Enough for 8–10 burritos.

Chilequiles

Tortilla Hash

For breakfast or lunch, a memorable dish that need never be made the same way twice. Basically, chilequiles are made with tortillas, sour cream, and cheese, but try varying the recipe with eggs, with red chiles and chorizo, with green chiles and chicken . . . whatever you have on hand!

24 tortillas (stale)
Lard or peanut oil
2 cups salsa verde (see p. 36)
1 cup chicken broth
2½ cups white cheese—Monterey Jack
  or Muenster
1 cup sour cream or crema (see p. 210)

Tear the tortillas into ½-inch strips and fry them in hot oil or lard (don't let them get crisp). Drain on paper towels. When all tortillas are fried, pour off remaining fat in the pan and add the salsa verde and broth to heat. Stir in the tortilla strips, cheese, and sour cream to make a creamy hash. Spoon the mixture into shallow bowls and place under the broiler to bubble. Serve at once.

Serves 6.

Torta de Yucatán

Yucatán Tortilla Stack

The Sauce:
> 1 onion, minced
> ¼ cup oil
> 3 canned green chiles, diced
> 1 large can tomatoes or 6 fresh
> tomatoes, blanched, peeled, and
> chopped
> 1 teaspoon oregano
> Salt and pepper to taste

Sauté onion in oil until translucent. Add chiles and cook slowly. Add mashed tomato pulp, season with oregano, salt, and pepper, and cook slowly, covered, for 10 minutes.

> 10 tortillas
> Oil for frying
> 3 chorizos (if you cannot find or make
> the Mexican sausage, you can
> substitute 3 hot Italian sausages)
> 1 pound ground beef
> 1 clove garlic, peeled
> 1 pound Monterey Jack cheese, grated

Fry tortillas in oil lightly, and drain on thick paper towels. Skin chorizo and fry until crumbly. Set aside. Cook the ground meat in an uncovered skillet with barely enough water to cover. Add a peeled garlic clove to the water. When the water has cooked down, and the meat begins to brown, sauté until dry. Mix with the drained sausage.

In a casserole dish, place 1 tortilla at bottom and spread with meat mixture in an even layer. Add a layer of grated cheese and a few tablespoons of sauce. Place another tortilla on top, and repeat layers until you have used all 10 tortillas. End with a tortilla on the top. Dribble a thin layer of sauce and grate cheese over the entire stack.

Heat through in a preheated 350° oven. Serve by slicing into wedges like a layer cake.

Serves 6–8.

Gorditas

If you are desperate to find tortillas, and too timid to make your own, you can easily make their kissing cousin, the gordita. Even a clumsy-fingered cook can form a fat tortilla and do everything with it one would do with a machine-made or handmade tortilla.

Depending on their shape, gorditas are called *sopes*, round or oblong in shape; *chalupas*, little boats; *relojes*, pocket watches; or *sombreros*, little hats.

To keep it simple we'll start with a sope. Pat a ball of masa into a circle about 5 inches in diameter, or follow the contour of your hand and make an elongated circle. When you master that, you can change the shape by pinching the sides and forming a small canoe, or by pinching the sides and forming the brim of a sombrero, then puffing it up in the center to form the sombrero's crown.

The pocket watch is easy: just make a slight depression in a circle about 4 inches in diameter and slightly pinch up the sides. When they are cooked, you can put filling in the dips in the brim of the sombrero or in the depression in the pocket watch. Be creative. Anything you put in them will taste good—as long as the salsa topping is *picante*.

Gorditas

Fat little tortillas like those you'll find in the mercados and on the street stands.

The Dough:
> 2 cups masa harina
> 1⅓ cups warm water

Mix the flour and water together to make a soft dough. Take a small piece of dough and roll it into a ball about 2 inches in diameter. Flatten it in the tortilla press or roll it into an oblong circle between 2 pieces of waxed paper or 2 sandwich bags.

Cook lightly on one side in a comal or griddle, then turn, and as you cook the second side pinch up the sides to make a shallow wall to hold the filling and the sauce. Flip it back on the first side and cook the dough a little longer.

These can be made ahead of time; just before serving fry them lightly in oil. Fill with a layer of frijoles refritos (see p. 159), a spoonful of fried and crumbled chorizo, and a sprinkling of grated cheese and shredded lettuce. Or simply fill with grated white cheese and top with salsa verde (see p. 36) or salsa cruda (see p. 29) and sour cream. Or fill with shredded chicken or meat, shredded lettuce, and radish slices, and top with salsa ranchera (see p. 32).

An excellent filling for relojes is finely minced spinach sautéed briefly with finely minced shrimp, fresh or dried, with a dusting of chili powder and garlic pepper.

Makes 12.

Tamales

Tamales are a fiesta food. In Mexico, they are served on every festive occasion: Christmas, New Year's, saints' days, national holidays, and weddings. Their origin dates back to Montezuma's time and before him to the ancient Aztecs.

At Christmas in our home, my youngest daughter always decides the day she's going to make tamales. Then she enlists all the help she can muster, just as it is done in Mexico. The servants, friends, and, of course, all members of the family are pressed into service.

My job is to make the filling and do the chopping, shredding, and stirring. She soaks the corn husks, brings home the masa already prepared with lard from our favorite Mexican *grocetería*. For two hundred tamales she orders nine pounds of masa and brings a stockpot to carry it home. And then, with or without help, she fills the corn husks with the filling I have concocted and ties them into neat little packages for steaming and then freezing, if we're not about to eat all two hundred at once.

The smell of corn husks and masa steaming with a pungent combination of chiles and chicken or turkey, added to the scent of pine and evergreens, permeates our Christmas mood.

And there is nothing quite like the first taste of the test tamale from the steamer.

If you can get masa at your nearby Mexican market, you'll have an easy time of it. But for those who can't, following is the recipe for making the tamal dough with masa harina.

If you are able to buy the prepared masa already laced with lard, allow five pounds for every one hundred tamales. There's no reason to go to all the trouble of making them unless you make them by the hundreds, and they do freeze well.

Tamal Dough:
> ½ *pound lard*
> 2 *cups masa harina*
> 1½ *cups cold water*
> 1 *teaspoon salt*
> ¾ *cup lukewarm chicken or beef*
> *broth*

In the food processor or by hand, beat the lard for 5 minutes. Combine masa harina, cold water, and salt to make a dough. Mix dough with the lard and add broth, a little at a time, as you mix.

The corn husks that you buy dry and packaged will be tough and papery. Soak them in hot water for several hours or overnight, then shake them well and pat dry on paper towels.

To make the tamales, spread a thin film of tamal dough inside the broadest part of the corn husk, an area about 3 inches wide by 4 or 5 inches long. Spread the filling down the middle of the dough.

Fold the sides of the husks firmly. To tie them into tight waterproof packets, use thin strips torn from several husks. If you find this awkward, use pieces of string cut in 5-inch lengths.

To cook the tamales, fill a conventional steamer with water up to the level indicated and bring to a boil (if you don't have a steamer, place a strainer in a large soup kettle and stack the tamales in it). Stack the tamales upright in the steaming pot and cover them with corn husks. Cover tightly and keep the water beneath them at a boil. From time to time, you may have to replenish the boiling water.

Steam them for 1½ hours, then test. The dough should come away solidly from the husks.

They are delicious when eaten right out of the husks— when refrigerated or frozen, they can be heated in a 350° oven for 30 minutes or placed back in the steamer.

Fillings for Tamales:
Fillings for tamales can be the same as for enchiladas, or varied in numerous ways.

Poached and shredded chicken with mole sauce (see p. 40)
Monterey Jack cheese or mozzarella with strips of fresh green chiles (a simple filling)
Ground beef in red chile sauce (see p. 34) with the addition of raisins plumped in brandy
Pork and salsa verde (see p. 36)
Fresh green corn cut from the cob and mixed with canned peeled chiles (to create the classic tamal con elote)

Tamales dulces, the sweet tamales served for tea or dessert, are another classic Mexican dish. Just mix sugar, cinnamon, and raisins with the tamal dough and steam in corn husks as described.

Tamal de Cazuela con Pollo

Tamale Casserole with Chicken

*If you can find fresh masa, this tamale pie will be worth
the effort. Otherwise make a tortilla dough with 2 cups
of masa harina and 1⅓ cups of lukewarm water and mix
in 2 tablespoons of lard. Then follow the directions below.*

> 3 *large eggs, separated*
> ½ *pound fresh masa*
> 1 *cup whipping cream*
> ½ *cup soft butter*
> 1 *teaspoon baking powder*
> *Salt*

Beat egg whites until stiff and set aside. Blend masa and
whipping cream thoroughly, add butter, and beat well.
Add egg yolks 1 at a time. Add baking powder and salt,
and fold in egg whites.

The Filling:

> 2 *tablespoons oil or butter*
> 1 *small onion, chopped*
> 3 *large tomatoes, peeled and chopped*
> 1 *teaspoon oregano*
> ¼ *teaspoon cumin seeds*
> 1 *can peeled green chiles, chopped*
> 2 *cups cooked, cubed chicken or pork*
> 1 *cup pitted black olives, sliced*
> *Salt*
> *Grated Monterey Jack or cheddar*
>   *cheese*

Sauté onion in hot oil or butter; add tomatoes, oregano,
and cumin. Cook a few minutes then add chiles, chicken,
olives, and salt. Cook a few minutes more.

Place half the masa mixture at the bottom of a 2-quart casserole, top with filling, and cover with remaining masa. Bake 45 minutes in a 350° oven. Sprinkle with cheese and bake 15 minutes longer.

Serves 6.

Suggested Meat Fillings for Comidas Típicas

Chorizo

Chorizo (seasoned Mexican pork sausage) is to Mexican cuisine what ground beef is to the American table. If your nearby Mexican mercado or supermarket has chorizo in sausage casings, it can be very good, or it can be completely unreliable.

It is not difficult, however, to make your own, and you can freeze it in small packages to have on hand for all your cooking needs.

The two recipes for chorizo that follow differ in taste and the time of preparation, but both are good.

Chorizo a la Mexicana

Mexican Sausage

 1 *pound lean pork*
 1 *teaspoon salt*
 2 *tablespoons chili powder*
 1 *clove garlic, mashed*
 2 *teaspoons vinegar*
 1 *teaspoon oregano*

In a food grinder or a processor, grind the pork coarsely. Add all the other ingredients and let stand overnight.

Fry without adding fat for about 30 minutes. If you are not going to use all the chorizo right away, you can store the uncooked chorizo in a covered jar in the refrigerator, where it will keep for about a week. Cooked, it can be frozen in small portions for use as you need it.

Serves 6.

Chorizo de Toluca

Toluca Pork Sausage

> 3 pasilla chiles
> 2 ancho chiles
> ¼ cup tequila
> ½ cup water
> 2½ pounds boneless pork
> 1 teaspoon coriander seeds
> ½ teaspoon cumin seeds
> 1 teaspoon oregano
> 2 cloves garlic, minced
> 3 tablespoons paprika
> 1 teaspoon salt
> ½ cup vinegar

Toast the chiles lightly over a burner flame or in an un-greased skillet or comal. Do not brown. Core and seed them, and break them into pieces. Pour tequila and water to cover and let them sit overnight (or at least 6 hours).

Grind the pork in a meat processor, or let your butcher grind it for you (some of the fat should not be trimmed away). Puree the chile mixture and add it to the meat. Grind the coriander and cumin seeds (if you have a mortar and pestle, it will help) and add the spices to the pork. If you are less of a purist, you can buy the ground cumin and ground coriander. Add remaining ingredients and mix well. Freeze in ¼-pound packages and wrap well for freezing.

When ready to use in other recipes, fry in a small amount of oil until crisp, and add to other ingredients.

Makes 10 packages.

Pollo

Chicken

Use either 2 double chicken breasts (costlier, but easier to prepare) or 1 small roasting or frying chicken.

In a pot, place chicken or chicken breasts with enough water to cover, seasoned with salt and pepper. Add any of the following:

> *Celery, with tops left on*
> *Sliced onion*
> *Garlic cloves*
> *Bay leaf*

Bring water to a boil and simmer for about 35–45 minutes, until chicken is cooked through and tender.

Remove from broth (save broth for recipes needing chicken stock) and let chicken cool. Remove skin and pull meat off bones, shredding it with your fingers or with the tines of 2 forks.

Makes enough for 12 tortillas.

Puerco

Pork

> 2 *pounds pork butt*
> ½ *medium-sized onion, quartered*
> 1 *clove garlic*
> 1 *teaspoon salt*
> ¼ *teaspoon oregano*
> ¼ *teaspoon cumin*

Place pork butt in a large saucepan and add water to cover. Add onion, garlic, salt, oregano, and cumin. Bring to a boil. Reduce heat and simmer for 2 hours, covered.

Drain meat and place in a baking pan. Sprinkle with additional salt and bake in a preheated 350° oven for about 35 minutes.

When cool enough to handle, shred meat with the tines of 2 forks.

Makes about 4 cups.

Carne Machaca

Shredded Beef

Similar to ropa vieja (see p. 128), but made with tomatoes. Can be made with flank steak or with stewing beef.

> 2 *pounds boneless beef chuck, flank,*
>   *or stewing beef*
> 10 *peppercorns*
> ½ *onion, quartered*
> 2 *cloves garlic, mashed*
> *Salt to taste*
> ½ *onion, chopped*
> 2 *tomatoes, peeled, seeded, and*
>   *chopped*
> 3 *California chiles (or 1 3-oz. can),*
>   *peeled, seeded, and cut into thin*
>   *strips*

Place meat in a Dutch oven and cover with water. Add peppercorns, the quartered ½ onion, 1 clove garlic, and salt. Bring to a boil, then reduce heat and simmer, covered, until meat is tender—about 2 hours. Remove meat from broth. Reserve broth. When cool enough to handle, shred meat with the tines of 2 forks or with your fingers.

In a large skillet, heat enough oil to cover the bottom, add the other clove of garlic, the chopped half onion, and a sprinkling of salt. Cook until transparent but not browned. Add tomatoes and chiles, and continue to cook. Add meat, along with enough broth to keep it from becoming too dry. Add salt to taste.

Serve with tortillas or rice, or use as filling for burritos or enchiladas.

Makes 8 servings, or filling for 12 enchiladas.

Picadillo

Mexican Hash

> 1 tablespoon lard
> 1 clove garlic, peeled and chopped
> ½ medium-sized onion, finely chopped
> 2 medium-sized tomatoes, skinned, seeded, and finely chopped
> 1 teaspoon oregano
> 2 pounds ground beef
> 3 peeled green chiles, fresh or canned
> ½ cup blanched almonds
> ½ cup raisins plumped in brandy

Melt the lard and fry the garlic and onion without browning. Add the tomato and oregano, and fry for a minute or more. Add ground meat and continue to fry and cook over medium flame until tender. Stir in chiles, almonds, and raisins, and simmer for 30 minutes.

Makes 4 cups.

Steak and Chorizo Filling for Taquitos

> 1–1½ pounds flank steak
> 1 large potato, peeled
> 2–3 ounces chorizo (see p. 116)
> Oil for frying
> ½ onion, finely chopped
> 1 medium-sized tomato, blanched,
>   peeled, and chopped, or 1 (8-oz.)
>   can tomato puree
> Salt and pepper to taste

Place flank steak in a large saucepan or Dutch oven, cover with water, and bring to a boil. Reduce heat and simmer, covered, until tender—about 1 hour. Remove from broth, and when cool enough to handle, shred meat with fingers or tines of 2 forks.

In boiling water, cook potato, peeled but uncut, until tender (about 20 minutes). Cool, grate coarsely, and set aside.

Cook chorizo in a skillet until crumbly. Add onion and cook until tender. Add shredded meat, grated potato, and tomato sauce. Cook, stirring to mix flavors, for about 5 minutes.

Taste and correct seasoning.

Makes about 3 cups, enough for 2 dozen taquitos.

CHAPTER VII

𝕲𝕲𝕲𝕲𝕲𝕲𝕲𝕲𝕲𝕲𝕲𝕲𝕲𝕲𝕲𝕲𝕲𝕲𝕲𝕲𝕲𝕲𝕲𝕲𝕲𝕲

Meat and Chicken Entrees

𝕲𝕲𝕲𝕲𝕲𝕲𝕲𝕲𝕲𝕲𝕲𝕲𝕲𝕲𝕲𝕲𝕲𝕲𝕲𝕲𝕲𝕲𝕲𝕲𝕲𝕲

Carne Asada

Grilled Steak

> 1 tender steak per person—club, New
>   York, or small sirloin
> Salt and pepper to taste
> Juice ½ lime
> Pinch chili powder

Steaks and all meats in Mexico are cut differently from our own, and the best way to prepare these steaks for the classic carne asada is to butterfly them.

Cut almost through the center of the steak, but not quite through the meat. Open each steak up and flatten it with a heavy cleaver. Season with salt and pepper, a squeeze of lime juice, and a sprinkling of chili powder.

Sear well on both sides on a hot griddle or in a heavy frying pan.

Serve with frijoles refritos (see p. 159), guacamole (see p. 43), and/or salsa picante (see p. 30), with warmed corn tortillas on the side.

Bistec con Chiles y Queso

Steak with Chiles and Cheese

> 3 *poblano chiles, fresh (or 1 small 4-oz.*
> *can green chiles)*
> *Oil for frying*
> 1 *clove garlic, minced*
> 1 *onion, sliced very thin*
> 8 *ounces Monterey Jack cheese, thinly*
> *sliced*
> 6 *filet mignons, each sized for 1 serving*
> *(6–8 ounces)*
> *Salt and pepper to taste*

Prepare fresh chiles by placing on gas burner or under broiler until skin blisters. Wrap in wet paper towels, and when cool enough to handle, remove blistered skin. Slit open and remove seeds, veins, and stems. If using canned chiles, slit and remove seeds and veins. Cut into thin slices lengthwise.

In a saucepan, heat enough oil for frying, and sauté the garlic and onion. Add the chile pieces and stir together, then remove from the heat. Add the cheese and let it melt into the chiles and onions, but do not cook.

Take each filet and butterfly it (cut through the center

without cutting all the way through, and open it sand-wich-style). Pound to flatten and season lightly with salt and pepper. Spoon the cheese mixture onto one side of the filet and fold over the other side as a top, pressing the edges together lightly to seal cheese inside. Barbecue or broil quickly and serve with salsa picante (see p. 30).

Serves 6.

Adobo Abuelito

Steak with Red Chiles

On the ranch, my grandfather used to coat flank steaks with dried chile pulp and hang them with wooden clothespins on the line in the sun. The collection of steaks were sun-drying long after the sheets and under-wear that hung beside them were taken in.

I treat my own steaks indoors before barbecuing or broiling them, but I season them in much the same way he did.

> 2 *cloves garlic, very finely chopped*
> 1 *cup chile pulp, or 4 tablespoons chili powder, preferably pasilla chile*
> 1 *flank steak, ½–2 pounds*

Mix the garlic with the pulp of the pasilla chile (softened and pureed in a blender) or with the pasilla powder. Coat the steak on one side, and place it face up under the broiler until the chile has been seared into the steak (4–7 minutes). Then turn and coat the underside, and broil the final side until it is nicely browned.

Do not overcook.

Serves 4.

Bistec a la Mexicana

Mexican Skirt Steak

Skirt steak, if you can find it in the market, is a delicate and tasteful cut of meat.

Marinate the steak in lime juice or red wine for about an hour (the Mexicans always soak it in vinegar, which I find too biting). Dust with red chili powder and finely minced garlic, broil quickly on both sides, and serve with warmed tortillas.

Puntas de Filete Entomatado

Sirloin Tips in Fresh Tomato Sauce

> 4 tablespoons olive oil
> 2 pounds beef sirloin cut in bite-sized
>   pieces
> Salt and paprika
> 3 tablespoons sweet butter
> ½ cup minced green onions
> 2 cloves garlic, mashed
> 6 tomatoes, peeled, seeded, and
>   chopped
> 1 cup double rich beef broth (see p. 55)
> 3 tablespoons minced parsley
> 2 teaspoons oregano
> 2 serrano chiles, seeded and minced
> ½ glass sherry

Heat oil in heavy skillet and add meat. Brown meat lightly over medium heat and salt lightly. Dust heavily with paprika and stir. Add butter, onions, and garlic, and sauté for 5 minutes. Add tomatoes, broth, parsley, oregano, and chiles. Cover and simmer over a low heat for 15 minutes. Remove cover, increase heat to medium-high, and reduce sauce until it is thick and well blended. Add salt to taste and sherry.

Serve with rice or beans.

Serves 4–6.

Chile Verde and Beef

A Mexican Beef Stroganoff

> 2 *pounds round or flank steak, cut into*
> *thin strips*
> *Paprika or pasilla chili powder*
> ¼ *cup oil*
> 6 *tomatoes, peeled and seeded, or*
> 1 *(28-oz.) can Italian tomatoes*
> 2 *tablespoons lemon juice*
> 1 *clove garlic, crushed*
> 1 *teaspoon ground cumin*
> *Pinch salt*
> 1 *medium-sized green pepper,*
> *chopped*
> 3 *green onions, chopped*
> ⅓ *cup chopped parsley*
> ½ *cup beef broth*
> 1 *(4-oz.) can green chiles, diced*

Cut the steak into ¼-inch strips (easier to do if partially frozen). Dust the meat with paprika or chili powder and brown in a heavy skillet in hot oil. Do not crowd the pan;

brown half the meat at a time if necessary. Pour off any excess oil. If using canned tomatoes, drain liquid and reserve. Cut tomatoes into pieces and set aside. Add lemon juice, tomato liquid, garlic, cumin, and a dash of salt to the meat and stir. Then stir in green pepper, onions, and parsley. Add broth to mixture and cover tightly, cooking on a low flame for 30 minutes. Add tomatoes and chiles and cook for 15 minutes longer.

Pass a bowl of sour cream to add if desired. Excellent with arroz blanca (see p. 162).

Serves 4–6.

Ropa Vieja

Shredded Beef with Chiles

"Old Clothes," as this shredded beef dish is called, can be made in advance and reheated. Serve with warmed flour tortillas or use as a filling for burritos, beef enchiladas, and other tortilla dishes.

> 1½ *pounds flank steak*
> 1 *cup water*
> 4 *cloves garlic, crushed*
> 4 *peppercorns*
> Salt *to taste*
> ¼ *cup vegetable oil*
> 1 *medium-sized onion, cut into thin slices*
> 4 *fresh California chiles, or 1 (3-oz.) can*

Place flank steak in a large, heavy Dutch oven. Add water, 3 garlic cloves, peppercorns, and salt. Heat until water comes to a boil. Reduce heat and simmer, covered, until meat is well done (about 1½–2 hours).

When meat is cooked and tender, remove from liquid and cool. When cool enough to handle, pull into fine shreds with fingers or the tines of 2 forks. Return shredded meat to the cooking water.

In a separate skillet, heat oil and the remaining garlic clove. Sauté, stirring constantly. Add onions and cook with garlic until transparent but not browned.

Add chiles, cut into strips. (If using fresh chiles, roast to remove skins. Remove seeds and stems, and cut into strips.) Add to skillet and continue stirring.

With a slotted spoon, transfer onions, chiles, and garlic to the Dutch oven containing meat and liquid, and cook uncovered for about 10 minutes.

Correct seasoning and serve with flour tortillas.

Makes 6 servings.

Albóndigas con Chiles

Meat Balls with Chile

> 1 *pound ground beef*
> ½ *pound ground pork*
> 2 *slices bread, soaked in hot milk and drained*
> 1 *egg, beaten*
> *Salt and pepper to taste*
> 2 *tablespoons oil*
> 1 *cup red chile sauce (comes in a can like enchilada sauce)*

Thoroughly mix meat, bread, egg, salt, and pepper. Form into meat balls about 2 inches in diameter. Heat oil in a skillet and add red chile sauce. Add meat balls to the sauce and cook, covered, over a low flame, for 45 minutes. If sauce becomes too dry or scant, add about ½ cup water.

Serves 4-6.

Albóndigas en Salsa de Almendra

Meat Balls in Almond Sauce

A festive and welcome addition to a holiday Mexican buffet.

> ¼ *small onion, finely minced*
> *Oil for frying*
> ¼ *cup tomato puree*
> 1 *cup water*
> ½ *cup blanched almonds*
> 1 *clove garlic*
> 3 *slices bread*
> 1 *cup hot milk*
> ¾ *pound ground beef*
> ¾ *pound ground pork*
> 1 *egg, beaten*
> *Salt and pepper to taste*

Fry onion in a tablespoon of oil. Add tomato puree and thin with about a cup of water. In another skillet, sauté almonds in 2 tablespoons of oil with the garlic clove and 1 slice of bread, torn into a few pieces. When bread is browned, remove garlic, almonds, and bread, and cool. Grind in a food processor to the consistency of a paste. Dilute if necessary and add to the tomato puree.

To make meat balls, soak 2 slices of bread in hot milk. Drain and add to the meat. Add beaten egg, salt, and pepper and mix thoroughly. Roll into small balls and add to the heated tomato-almond sauce. You may need to add more water. Cover tightly and cook meat balls for 30 minutes over a low flame.

Serves 6–8, or more on a buffet table.

Puerco en Mole Verde

Pork in Green Chile Sauce

> 3 *pounds pork, cut into cubes, or*
> 4 *pounds country-style pork*
> *spareribs*
> 1 *small onion, sliced*
> 2 *cloves garlic*
> *Salt to taste*
> ¼ *cup lard or oil*
> 2 *cups tomatillos, drained and rinsed*
> 5 *serrano chiles*
> 1 *cup seasoned broth (you can use*
> *broth that pork was cooked in)*
> *Sprigs parsley, cilantro, and watercress*

Place pork, onion, 1 clove of garlic, and salt in a large Dutch oven and add water to cover. Bring to a boil, lower flame, and simmer for 30 minutes.

In a separate pot, heat lard or oil. In a food processor or blender, combine tomatillos, other clove of garlic, and chiles to a smooth paste, then cook in the heated lard for about 10 minutes or until thickened. Add the seasoned broth and continue cooking.

Add the meat to the sauce and cook slowly for 1 hour.

At the last minute before serving, chop parsley, cilantro, and watercress either by hand or in a blender, and sprinkle together over the mole. Serve with rice or warmed tortillas.

Serves 6–8.

Mole de Olla

Mole from the Pot

An olla is the wide, open earthenware bowl that is used in every Mexican kitchen. When you find them, buy them in all sizes!

The Sauce:

> 6 *pasilla chiles*
> 3 *tablespoons lard or oil*
> 2 *tablespoons sesame seeds*
> 1 *medium-sized onion, chopped*
> 6 *medium-sized tomatoes, peeled,*
>   *seeded, and chopped, or 1 (28-oz.)*
>   *can Italian-style tomatoes*
> *Salt*

Soften chiles in water, then remove seeds and veins. Fry them in lard with the sesame seeds. Drain off any excess lard and run through blender or processor. In the same pan, wilt the onions in the lard and add tomatoes. Cook for 10 minutes, mashing down the tomatoes. Add the chile mixture and salt to taste.

5 pounds country-style pork
   spareribs, cut into serving pieces
1½ quarts water
1 bay leaf
2 mint leaves
6 whole peppercorns

Cook spareribs in water with seasonings until tender, at least 1 hour. Add sauce to the spareribs and broth. Cook for 30 minutes in the sauce, then take the pot to the table.

Serves 6–8.

Puerco en Adobo

Pork in Red Chile Sauce

4 ancho chiles
6 pasilla chiles
2 pounds pork, cut into cubes
Salt to taste
1 teaspoon marjoram
1 teaspoon thyme
6 peppercorns
5 cloves garlic, peeled and minced
1 onion, chopped
1 teaspoon cumin seed
2 tablespoons lard
2 bay leaves
Juice ½ lemon

Remove veins and seeds from chiles. Pour boiling water over them and let stand for 15 minutes to soften. Drain. Place pork in a saucepan and add water to cover. Season with salt, and bring to a boil. Reduce heat and simmer slowly until meat is tender (45–60 minutes). Drain, but save the cooking liquid.

Combine marjoram, thyme, peppercorns, garlic, onion, cumin, and salt. Blend the chiles in a blender jar and add to the spices.

Heat the lard in an earthenware casserole or heavy skillet and brown the pork lightly. Remove pork and set aside. In the same lard, cook the spice and chile mixture (the adobo), stirring constantly for about 10 minutes. Be careful not to burn sauce. When the sauce is thick enough to barely slide off the spoon, add 1 cup of the liquid in which the pork was cooked, the bay leaves, and the lemon juice. Add the meat and simmer another 10 minutes.

Serve with warm tortillas and salsa verde (see p. 36).

Serves 6.

Mole Poblano con Pollo o Guacalote

Chicken or Turkey Mole from Puebla

The grateful nuns from the Convent of Santa Rosa in Puebla are said to have created this most famous dish of Mexican cuisine to thank visiting dignitaries for funding a new wing of their convent. In their enthusiasm they took almost every item on their kitchen shelves and brought forth a multi-ingredient stew. Composed of chiles and chocolate and peanuts and raisins, this mole is wonderful with chicken or turkey and excellent as a sauce for enchiladas. The authentic Mexican recipe calls for more chocolate than we indicate; but that is a matter of preference. We also leave out the raisins, but that, too, is our personal taste.

10 *mulato chiles*
9 *pasilla chiles*
8 *ancho chiles*
⅓ *cup lard*
¼ *cup sesame seeds*
Pinch *anise seeds*
6 *coriander seeds*
10 *peppercorns*
6 *green tomatillos (fresh-cooked or canned)*
1 *large onion, chopped*
1 *clove garlic*
½ *cup ground almonds*
¼ *cup ground peanuts*
Chicken broth
¼ *circle Mexican chocolate, or 2 ounces bittersweet chocolate*
Salt to taste
1 *12-lb. turkey, quartered, or 2 5-lb. roasting chickens cut in eighths*
1 *tortilla, lightly toasted*
8 *tablespoons olive oil or butter*

Before cooking the chicken or turkey, rinse, seed, and devein the chiles. Fry lightly in a little lard, then cover with water and bring to a boil until puffed up. Let cool. Drain and put in the blender bowl. Toast the sesame and anise seeds for several minutes in an ungreased skillet, then add to the blended chiles with the remaining spices, tomatillos, and onions.

Fry a clove of garlic in a little more of the lard, add the ground almonds and peanuts, and stir to a paste. Add to the chiles in the blender along with a lightly toasted tortilla broken into pieces.

Cook this paste and stir in the remainder of the lard, then add all the blended ingredients. Add enough chicken broth to make a thick, smooth paste. Melt the chocolate in a double boiler and add to the mixture. Salt to taste.

The turkey pieces can be browned in a Dutch oven in olive oil, or can be placed in the oven, dotted with butter, and baked at 375° uncovered until slightly browned. After browning, cover with water. Cover tightly with foil, place in 300° oven. Leave for about 3 hours, then uncover, cool and remove turkey meat from the bones. Add to the mole and heat through. Serve with arroz blanca (see p. 162) or green rice with parsley.

If using chicken instead of turkey, brown the chicken lightly in olive oil, then cover with broth and simmer uncovered until the broth cooks down. Pour the mole sauce over the moistened chicken and heat through.

Serves 12–15.

Pollo con Pimientos Rojos

Chicken Breasts with Red Peppers

When sweet red peppers are in season, this is an easy and flavorful dish.

> 4 *whole chicken breasts*
> ½ *cup sherry*
> 2 *sweet red peppers, or 1 4-oz. can*
> *pimientos, sieved*
> 1 *(14½-oz.) can evaporated milk*
> *Salt and pepper to taste*
> 1 *cup coarsely grated Swiss cheese*
> *Parsley sprigs*

Poach the chicken breasts in sherry, covered, for 20 minutes. You may need to add a little water to keep them from sticking. Cool, and remove meat from bones. Place meat in a well-buttered shallow baking dish.

If using fresh peppers, toast them over the flame or in an ungreased skillet. Steam for 20 minutes in a tightly closed paper bag, then peel as much of the outer skin as you can. A bit of the scorched skin will not hurt the flavor. Slice into ½-inch strips.

Place the pepper strips over the separated breasts of chicken. Combine the milk, salt, and pepper, and pour over the chicken and peppers. Sprinkle the cheese on top and bake at 325° for 20 minutes. Garnish with parsley and serve with arroz verde (see p. 164).

Serves 6.

Pollo en Jugo de Naranja

Chicken à l'Orange

> 1 *roasting chicken left whole*
> 1 *cup cooked white rice*
> 2 *tablespoons rosemary*
> 1 *orange, peeled, and membrane*
>   *removed*
> ¼ *cup butter*
> 1 *cup orange juice*
> 1 *cup sherry*
> *Salt to taste*

Place chicken, breast down, on a rack in roasting pan.

Mix the rice and rosemary with segments of peeled orange. Add salt if desired.

Stuff the chicken with rice mixture, and seal with string or little skewers. Dot the top of the chicken with butter, and pour ½ cup orange juice and cup sherry over it. Bake for 35 minutes in a 350° oven. Turn, add a few more dots of butter, and baste with the remainder of the orange juice. Bake for 20 minutes longer or until the leg joints move easily and no pink flesh shows. Add salt to taste.

Serve with arroz Mexicana (see p. 163) (with peas and/or avocado) and colache (see p. 172). Or, if feeling festive, try wild rice—this dish deserves the royal treatment.

Serves 4–6.

Pollo Mazatlán

Chicken from Mazatlán

This recipe comes, reluctantly given to us by the chef, from an exclusive private club in Mazatlán.

> 2 tablespoons oil
> 3 green onions, chopped
> 1 (4-oz.) can green chile peppers, sliced
> 1 clove garlic, minced
> 2 cups tomatillos (canned), drained and rinsed
> 2 tablespoons flour
> 1 tablespoon sugar
> Salt to taste
> 1 cup chicken broth
> 6 chicken breasts, boned and halved
> 1 cup dry sherry
> 12 slices Monterey Jack or mozzarella cheese
> 6 sprigs parsley
> 6 sprigs cilantro

In a skillet, fry onions until translucent but not browned. Add the chiles, garlic, and tomatillos (which have been rinsed and drained). Stir and simmer for 10 minutes. Sprinkle with flour, sugar, and salt to taste and stir until absorbed. Add the broth and cook uncovered, stirring constantly, for another 5 minutes.

Poach the chicken breasts in the sherry, uncovered, for 35 minutes in a 350° oven. Place chicken breasts on an oven-proof plate and pour the sauce over them. Place a slice of cheese on each breast and turn oven up higher, placing plate with chicken in the oven until the cheese melts.

Garnish with sprigs of parsley and cilantro.

Serves 6.

Guisado de Pollo

Chicken Fricassee Mexicana

> 5 pounds assorted chicken parts
> 4 tablespoons olive oil
> ½ pound ham, cubed
> ¼ pound Mexican chorizos (see p. 116)
> 1 #2 can solid-pack tomatoes
> 1 clove garlic, mashed
> 1 medium-sized onion, minced
> ½ cup minced parsley
> ½ cup toasted and pulverized almonds
> ½ teaspoon rosemary
> ½ cup dry sherry

Brown the chicken in oil. Add ham and chorizo sausage that has been taken from the casings and fry until the chorizo is well cooked. Add tomatoes, garlic, onion, parsley, almonds, and rosemary and simmer for 30 minutes. Then transfer to a baking dish, add sherry, and heat in a 350° oven for 30 minutes.

Serve with arroz blanca (see p. 162) sprinkled with chopped parsley.

Serves 10–12.

Arroz con Pollo

Chicken with Rice

1 *cup raw rice*
1 *5-lb. chicken, cut in pieces*
½ *stick butter*
1 *medium-sized onion, minced*
1 *clove garlic, minced*
4 *medium-sized tomatoes, peeled, seeded, and mashed*
½ *cup cubed raw ham, or 2 Italian-style sausages, sliced*
½ *sweet red pepper, chopped, or 1 small can of pimientos*
3 *cups chicken broth*
1 *bay leaf*
1 *teaspoon epazote*
1 *teaspoon rosemary*
1 *tablespoon chopped parsley*
¼ *cup peas*

Cover rice with boiling water and set aside for 15 minutes. Simmer the chicken in water to cover for 45 minutes. Remove chicken from the broth and when cool, remove meat from the bone in fairly large pieces.

Drain rice and rinse in several washings, then simmer in butter until translucent. Add onion and garlic. Stir well. Add tomato pulp, ham or sausages, and red pepper or pimiento. Pour in 3 cups chicken broth, the herbs and parsley, and cover tightly. In 20 minutes add the chicken and simmer until all liquid has disappeared. Just before serving add the peas and heat until cooked (about 5 minutes).

Serve with fresh salsa roja (see p. 34) and/or fresh salsa verde (see p. 36).

Serves 4–6.

Mancha Manteles

Tablecloth Stainer

This is a classic Mexican dish that uses the macho, *a firm-fleshed variety of banana found in Mexico. You can make it with regular bananas, but they must be added at the last minute.*

The Sauce:

    1 tablespoon blanched almonds
    1 teaspoon sesame seeds
    Cooking oil
    1 onion, chopped
    1 green pepper, chopped
    1 (8-oz.) can tomato sauce
    1 tablespoon chili powder
    ¼ cup sugar
    3 whole cloves
    ½ teaspoon cinnamon
    1 bay leaf
    Salt and pepper to taste

Brown almonds and sesame seeds in a small amount of oil and add onion and green pepper, sautéing until soft but not brown. Add tomato sauce, chili powder, sugar, cloves, cinnamon, and bay leaf. Cook for 10 minutes, adding water if sauce becomes too dry. Remove bay leaf and cloves and puree in blender. Taste and correct seasoning.

> 1 *pound lean pork, cut into small*
> *cubes*
> *Oil for frying*
> 1 *roasting chicken, cut into pieces*
> *Flour*
> *Salt and pepper*
> 1 *sweet potato, cut into cubes*
> 1 *tart apple, peeled, cored, and cut*
> *into cubes*
> 2 *bananas, sliced*

Brown pork in skillet in hot oil and remove to a large saucepan or Dutch oven. Dust chicken pieces with flour seasoned with salt and pepper, and brown in the same oil that the pork was cooked in. Add chicken to pork. Pour sauce over meat.

Add sweet potato and simmer for another 15 minutes. Then add apple and simmer for a few minutes longer.

When ready to serve, slice bananas into the hot stew and serve in large soup bowls—with plenty of napkins.

Serves 8.

Pozole

Pork Stew

In Mexico, pozole is usually served after a parranda, a big night on the town. A cross between a stew and a soup, it is also a wonderful dish to serve in soup bowls after a football game or on a cold winter night with friends. The true pozole is made with a pig's head and pig's feet, but I like this adapted version, made with chicken, pork, and beef, even better.

1 pound beef chuck, cut into cubes
1 chicken, cut into eighths
1 pound pork loin, cut into cubes
Cooking oil
1 medium-sized onion, chopped
2 cloves garlic, mashed
3 quarts water
Salt to taste
1 pound hominy (#2½ can)
3 tablespoons chili powder, or
    6 tablespoons chile pulp—
    combination of any red chiles

Brown separately the beef, chicken, and pork, each in enough oil to brown lightly. Put together in a deep pot with the onion and garlic and salted water and cook until meats are tender. Add the hominy and chile pulp or powder, and continue cooking for about 45–60 minutes.

Serve pozole in large soup bowls with hot tortillas on the side.

Prepare bowls of garnishes—chopped green onions, shredded lettuce, oregano, and sliced radishes. Offer chopped fresh jalapeños for the hardy.

Serves 8–10.

CHAPTER VIII

Fish and Seafood Entrees

Huachinango Veracruz

Baked Red Snapper

The red snapper, if available, is a wonderful fish that, when cooked properly, has the texture of lobster. In Veracruz, the whole fish is cooked with chiles, lemons, and tomatoes, and makes a beautiful presentation. If only filets are available, the recipe can be varied to accommodate the smaller pieces of fish. But do try to cook and serve it whole.

1 2–3 *pound whole red snapper,*
   cleaned
2 *lemons, thinly sliced*
Butter or olive oil
2 *tomatoes, sliced*
1 *green pepper, sliced into rings*
6 *strips canned green chiles*
1 *yellow onion, sliced*
Salt and pepper to taste
Green olives, stuffed with pimientos
   (*optional*)
Capers (*optional*)

Rub the cleaned fish inside and out with a cut lemon. Place in a shallow baking dish that has been dotted with butter or coated with cooking oil. Cover the fish with slices of tomato, rings of green pepper, strips of green chile, thin slices of lemon, and onion. Salt and pepper to taste.

Dribble a bit of olive oil over the top, or dot with butter. Bake for 30 minutes in preheated 350° oven, or until fish flakes easily with a fork.

Garnish with olives and capers. Serve with salsa verde (see p. 36) on the side.

Serves 6.

Pescado a la Veracruzana

Fish from Veracruz

A variation of the classic Huachinango Veracruz, this would normally be made with the omnipresent red snapper. But any firm white-fleshed fish is suitable.

> 1 large onion, chopped
> 3 tablespoons olive oil
> Salt and pepper to taste
> 6 medium-sized tomatoes, peeled, seeded, and chopped
> 2 pounds red snapper or bass
> 2 tablespoons capers
> 1 jar (3-oz.) pimientos, coarsely chopped
> 6–8 green olives

Simmer onion in olive oil until translucent. Add tomatoes and season with salt and pepper. Cook until tomatoes are soft.

Place the fish in a buttered baking dish, or one that is coated with cooking oil. Add the capers and pimientos, but hold the olives. Pour tomato sauce over the fish and bake at 350° for 30 minutes, or until fish flakes easily with a fork. Add olives the last 10 minutes of cooking time.

Serves 4–6.

Huachinango Las Hadas

Red Snapper in Parsley Sauce

The fabulous white Arabian-like resort, Las Hadas, presides over an active port that has the freshest fish for miles around. This red snapper recipe is quick, easy to make, and equally good with any white fish that is available.

> 1 (13-oz.) can tomatillos
> 1 small onion, finely chopped
> 1 clove garlic, mashed
> 2 cups parsley, loosely packed
> Juice of 1 lime or ½ lemon
> Olive oil
> 4 large snapper filets (or similar white
>   fish)
> Pickled jalapeño chiles, sliced
> Salt and freshly ground pepper to taste

Drain and rinse tomatillos, and run through blender until smooth. Add onions, garlic, parsley, and lime or lemon juice, and continue blending. Heat the sauce in a small amount of olive oil. Place the fish fillets in a shallow baking dish or open casserole, and pour the heated sauce over the fish. Top with a scattering of sliced chiles. Add salt and freshly ground pepper. Bake uncovered in a 475° oven for about 15 minutes, or until fish flakes easily with a fork.

Serve with lemon wedges and arroz blanca (see p. 162).

Serves 4.

Pescado en Salsa
de Jitomate y Cilantro

Fish in Tomato and Coriander Sauce

> ¼ cup olive oil
> 2 swordfish steaks (or halibut or
>   similar firm fish), totaling about
>   3 pounds
> 2 ripe tomatoes, peeled, seeded, and
>   chopped
> 1 onion, chopped
> 1 clove garlic, minced
> ½ head romaine lettuce (or heart of
>   romaine)
> 2 teaspoons fresh cilantro
> 1 (4-oz.) can pimientos
> 1 cup bottled clam juice
> Salt and pepper to taste
> Avocado slices to garnish

Using a skillet, brown fish lightly on both sides in olive oil. Remove fish and place in an oven-proof casserole. Place tomatoes, onion, garlic, lettuce, cilantro, pimiento, and clam juice in a food processor or blender and puree. Taste and correct seasoning with salt and pepper.

Place pureed sauce in the skillet in which fish was browned and heat in the oil for about 5 minutes, stirring constantly. Pour sauce over the fish and simmer gently over low heat until fish flakes easily. Lift gently onto a warmed serving plate and garnish with avocados.

Serves 6.

Pescado en Adobo

Fish in Adobo Sauce

> 6 ancho chiles, or 6 tablespoons
>   dried red chili powder
> 1 whole 5-lb. sea bass, red snapper,
>   or striped bass
> Flour, salt, and pepper
> ½ cup olive oil
> 1 onion, chopped
> 1 clove garlic, minced
> ⅛ teaspoon ground clove
> ¼ teaspoon cinnamon
> ¼ teaspoon oregano
> ¼ teaspoon cumin
> ½ teaspoon thyme
> 3 large tomatoes, peeled, seeded,
>   and chopped
> Lemon juice
> ¼–½ cup grated Parmesan cheese
> Butter

If using fresh ancho chiles, soak in hot water for about an hour, after having removed all seeds, stems, and veins. Cut into inch-long pieces and puree in a blender along with the water in which they were soaked.

Dust fish with flour seasoned with salt and pepper. Sauté in olive oil until golden on both sides. Place in a large greased oven-proof dish and keep warm.

In a blender or food processor, combine prepared chiles (or powdered chili), onions, garlic, clove, cinnamon, oregano, cumin, thyme, and tomatoes until coarsely pureed. Adjust seasoning with salt and pepper to taste. Heat the sauce in a skillet with about 2 tablespoons of olive oil. Cook for about 5 minutes, stirring constantly.

Add about 3 tablespoons of lemon juice and continue stirring.

Pour the sauce over fish in the casserole. Sprinkle with cheese and dot with butter.

Bake in a preheated oven at 400° for about 40 minutes, or until fish flakes easily.

Serve with boiled potatoes.

Serves 6.

Langosta con Frijoles Refritos

Lobster with Refried Beans

I remember stopping as a child at the Rosarita Beach Hotel on the way to the races at Agua Caliente. Everyone who was anyone in Hollywood would lunch there on the way to the popular racetrack—Charlie Chaplin, Marion Davies, Gilbert Roland, Rudolph Valentino, and Pola Negri. Elegant and luxurious touring cars—Auburns, Pierce-Arrows, Marmons, and Lincolns—would be parked in front of the hotel.

Years later, my husband and I sat in the somewhat seedy but still romantic palm-decorated bar, and I ordered lobster and refried beans for dinner. My husband thought I had lost my mind, until he tasted the combination and agreed that refried beans go with everything and make everything taste superb.

Allow ½ lobster tail or full Maine lobster per person. Lobster should be fresh, halved, and dotted with butter and parsley.

Run lobster under the broiler, about 2–3 minutes, until the butter froths and the shell turns a bit brown.

Serve on the same dish with the frijoles refritos (see p. 159).

Camarónes al Ajillo

Shrimp in Chile and Garlic

    4 *dried California chiles*
1½ *cups olive oil*
    6 *cloves garlic, minced*
   ¼ *teaspoon sugar*
1¾ *pounds jumbo shrimp, in shells*
    2 *fresh green chiles (California or*
        Anaheim)
      White vinegar
      Salt (optional)

Cut off the ends and tops of the dried chiles. Remove and discard seeds. Cut chiles crosswise into ¼-inch rings. Place in a large bowl with olive oil, garlic, and sugar. Stir occasionally and marinate, tightly covered, at room temperature for several hours or overnight.

Slit shrimp through the shells down the center of the backs and remove veins with the tip of a knife. Leave shells on and rinse well in water and white vinegar to remove the "slime." Pat dry with paper towels and set aside.

Cut off stem ends of fresh chiles. Remove veins and seeds, and cut chiles crosswise into ¼-inch rings.

Heat dry chiles and marinate in a heavy skillet over medium heat. Add the fresh California chiles and the shrimp. Sauté, turning shrimp once, until shells turn pink and shrimp are firm to the touch. Add salt if desired and serve.

Serves 6.

Calamares (Squid)

Lovers of squid are like members of a cult. Once tried and liked, squid in its many forms can become an addiction. If you can't buy squid already cleaned from your fish market you'll find it's not hard to do it yourself. In fact, it is easier to clean squid than any other fish or shellfish.

Hold the body in one hand and pull off the tentacles (be sure to save them). Remove the skin and the fins. Reach inside and remove the fan-shaped cartilage—it will come out very easily. Then hold the squid under running water and remove any inner fatty wastes. Dry with paper towels. If you have trouble removing the skins from the tentacles you can parblanch them for 1–2 minutes, then plunge them into cold water to prevent further cooking.

Calamares Almendrados

Squid in Sherried Almond Sauce

> 2 medium-sized onions, chopped
> 1 clove garlic, minced
> 3 tablespoons olive oil
> ¼ pound blanched almonds
> ½ cup dry sherry
> 2 pounds squid, cut in rings
> 2 tablespoons minced parsley
> Pinch oregano
> Salt to taste

In a shallow casserole, sauté the onions and garlic in the oil until the onion is wilted. Grind almonds to a paste in a processor and gradually add the sherry. Place the squid in the casserole with the onions and garlic. Add the parsley, oregano, and salt.

Pour the almond-sherry mixture over the squid. Cover and cook over a low flame until squid is tender (about 45 minutes).

Serve with rice and warm bolillos.

Serves 4–6.

Calamares en Su Tinta

Squid in Its Own Ink

The idea of squid served in a dark, almost black liquid may be unnerving to the uninitiated, but the squid's own ink gives this classic dish a subtle flavor that those who brave it for the first time just may find captivating.

> 2 pounds small squid
> 1 pound large squid (used only for the ink)
> ½ cup red wine
> 2 tablespoons olive oil
> 1 medium-sized onion, chopped
> 1 clove garlic, minced
> 1 tomato, peeled, seeded, and chopped
> 1 tablespoon minced parsley
> 1 tablespoon flour
> 1 cup chicken broth or clam juice
> Salt and freshly ground pepper

Clean the small squid, then slice into ½-inch rings. Cut up the tentacles (really the best part). Set aside.

Place the ink sacs of the large squid in a strainer and press them with a wooden spoon to extract the ink. Pour ¼ cup wine through the strainer. Set aside.

Heat the oil in a skillet and sauté the onion and garlic until the onion is translucent. Add the tomato and parsley and cook 5 minutes. Stir in the flour and mix well, then add the broth or clam juice and remaining wine. Pour in the ink mixture. The sauce should be black. If you didn't have enough ink, it will be brownish, but the flavor will still be fine. Season with salt and pepper. Add the squid rings and tentacles, and cook, covered, for 2 hours. To assure its tenderness, add a piece of cork to the cooking liquid (an old chef's trick).

Serve with arroz blanca (see p. 162).

Serves 4–6 aficionados.

Ostiónes

Oysters

From the Gulf of Mexico come the finest oysters. But Atlantic or Pacific oysters will do nicely.

> 12 oysters
> 2 tablespoons butter
> Pinch oregano
> Salt and pepper
> 4 strips green chile

Place the oysters in a buttered cazuela or ramekin. Add butter, pinch of oregano, salt, and pepper, and lay the strips of green chile across the top. Oyster liquid or water may be added if the oysters seem dry.

Bake in a preheated 400° oven until oysters plump up and edges begin to curl (about 10 minutes).

Serve with rounds of French rolls or bolillos fried in butter. Or better yet, serve 2 oysters in a hollowed-out bolillo and pour the buttery liquid over them. A Mexican version of Diamond Jim's favorite oyster loaf.

If you are serving real oyster lovers, the above recipe may just serve 2 of you. For an appetizer, it will probably serve 4.

◳◳◳◳◳◳◳◳◳◳◳◳◳◳◳◳◳◳◳◳◳◳◳◳◳◳◳◳◳

CHAPTER IX

Vegetables

◳◳◳◳◳◳◳◳◳◳◳◳◳◳◳◳◳◳◳◳◳◳◳◳◳◳◳◳◳

Beans

Rice

Vegetables and Side Dishes

Frijoles (Beans)

One of the wonders of the Mexican meal, for breakfast, lunch, or dinner, is the ever-present bowl of frijoles. From Monday through Sunday, the cazuela of beans is on a slow burner or in the oven, being heated or reheated. Delicious in many forms, the versatile dish appears, most frequently, as frijoles refritos, or refried beans.

There are many ways to combine beans with other

dishes. They go with everything from meat to chicken to lobster (in fact, with any fish). They can be enhanced with herbs, with wines, with sour cream, with a topping of fried chorizo, green peppers, or cheese.

Once you have mastered the Mexican method of cooking beans, you'll never want to open up another can of kidney beans—although they are a good substitute. Try cooking either Mexican pink beans (habichuelas rosadas), or pinto beans from scratch. It's an art, but all it takes is time, an occasional bit of stirring, a watchful eye, and a good imagination for experimenting.

In this country, the pink beans and the pinto beans need not be soaked before cooking, but they should be rinsed and picked over for any imperfections. In a Mexican household, the ever-present pot of beans moves through the entire week in a variety of forms:

On Monday, the beans would probably be basic, starting the week with the recipe for frijoles sencilla (see p. 158). The Mexican cook might make only the two cups called for in the recipe, but more than likely would make larger quantities to carry her through the week.

Tuesday's beans would be made from Monday's leftovers, and might result in the classic frijoles refritos (see p. 159), the classic refried beans served in every Mexican restaurant.

By Wednesday, any leftover refried beans might be topped with cubed yellow or white cheese, and heated until the cheese melts. A delicious and hearty side dish at any meal.

If anything were left of the humble frijoles that were begun on Monday, it might well form the base for a delicious tostada, or be wrapped in a warm flour tortilla to make a bean burrito.

By Friday, it would be time to start again, this time perhaps using the flavorful recipe for frijoles con jitomate y chile verde (see p. 159).

On Saturday, frijoles con chorizo (see p. 116) would greet hungry guests. A wonderful appetizer served with totopas (corn chips) or warmed tortillas and a pitcher of margaritas!

For Sunday dinner, the Mexican cook would quite possibly prepare a special dish of black beans to serve at a family gathering. The Cuban cook would serve the black beans together with white rice (see p. 161), and call the dish Cristianos y Moros.

Frijoles Sencilla

Basic Beans

Monday's beans are basic. Start the week with 2 cups of pink or pinto beans. Wash thoroughly, then drain and put in a skillet to cook with ¼ cup lard or cooking oil. When well coated with the oil, stir gently and add 5 cups of lukewarm water. Cover lightly and let simmer for 1½ hours. Look occasionally to see if more water should be added, but only add 1 scant cup at a time. Add salt and a little more lard the last 30 minutes of cooking.

In a heavy skillet heat ½ cup lard or cooking oil. Drain some of the beans, but save the liquid and add the beans to the heated fat. Mash with a wooden Mexican bean masher or a metal potato masher. Then add more liquid and more beans and repeat the procedure until all the beans and all the liquid have been used. Continue cooking over a low burner, stirring frequently until the beans are well mashed and tender.

The more lard you add, the richer the beans will be. Let your calorie count be your guide.

Frijoles Refritos

Refried Beans

Prepare frijoles sencilla (see p. 158). Heat 2 tablespoons of oil, lard, or bacon grease in a skillet. Add mashed beans and cook, stirring until the beans are completely dry. If the beans become too dry, the addition of 1 cup of sweet cream will make the dish richer and tastier.

Note: Refried beans will have a different flavor if you substitute vino rojo for the cream. Or, in states where beer is made, like Tecate or Nuevo Leon, the last minute addition would be beer. Rum, too, can dress up the dish.

Frijoles con Jitomate y Chile Verde

Beans with Tomato and Green Pepper

2 cups pink beans
5 cups lukewarm water
¼ cup lard, or 4 tablespoons cooking oil
1 whole onion
1 teaspoon oregano
6 fresh tomatoes
1 green bell pepper, chopped
3 green onions, finely sliced

Let's start over with 2 cups pink beans and 5 cups lukewarm water. Add the lard (or oil) and onion (left whole) to the pot. Simmer, covered, for 1 hour. Sprinkle with oregano and add 2 tomatoes, peeled, seeded, and chopped. In another pan sauté 4 fresh, finely sliced tomatoes, the green pepper, and the green onions. When the bean liquid has cooked down, add the tomato, oregano, pepper, and onion mixture and cook for 1 hour longer. These beans should be tender and whole in a thick broth.

Serve as a side dish in small soup bowls with a few slices of green pepper on top. Pass bowls of chopped serrano peppers to the brave.

Serves 6.

Salsa de Frijoles

Bean Dip

> 1 *clove garlic, mashed*
> *Oil or lard*
> 2 *cups cooked pink beans*
> 1 *small can Mexican chile sauce*
> 3 *chorizos*
> 1 *cup grated cheese*
> 3 *tablespoons minced onion*

Sauté garlic in oil or lard, but do not brown. Add beans and mash thoroughly. Add ½ can Mexican chile sauce to moisten the beans.

In another pan take 3 chorizos from their casings and fry them until crisp. Usually chorizos have enough oil to cook them, but if too dry, add a bit more oil. When they are browned and crisp add the chorizos to the beans and mix to a paste. Add more sauce, or a little water if needed, to make the consistency of a dip. Sprinkle with grated cheese and minced onion and enjoy this with corn chips or warm tortillas—and a margarita!

Serves 6–8.

Frijoles Negros

Black Beans

> 2 cups black beans
> 4 cups water
> 1 whole onion
> ½ cup lard or cooking oil
> 3 green onions, chopped
> 1 jalapeño pepper, finely chopped
> 2 medium-sized tomatoes, peeled,
>   seeded, and quartered
> 2 teaspoons oregano
> Salt and pepper to taste
> Salsa verde (see p. 36)

Wash beans well and drain. In 4 cups of lukewarm water cook the black beans and the onion for at least 2 hours. Black beans may need a longer cooking time than pink beans. When tender, turn the beans into a skillet in which you have fried the green onions and the jalapeño pepper. Add the tomatoes and simmer for 20 minutes until well blended. Add oregano and salt and pepper to taste.

Serve these beans with salsa verde on the side.

For variation, turn a ring mold filled with fluffy white rice out onto a wide, round dish. In the center of the rice ring place a mound of black beans. Pass the salsa verde. Cuban cooks call this dish Cristianos y Moros (Moors and Christians).

Serves 6.

Rice

Arroz Blanca

Mexican White Rice

When the main dish is very piquant, white rice can be the perfect accompaniment.

> 2 cups white rice
> ⅓ cup oil
> ½ cup toasted blanched almonds,
>   coarsely ground or slivered
> Salt to taste
> 4 cups hot chicken broth

Place rice in a bowl and pour boiling water over it. Let stand for 15 minutes. Rinse under cold water 3 or 4 times until water is clear of starch. Heat the oil and stir in the rice until all the grains are well coated. Stir in almonds and salt and continue stirring until rice is dry. Pour in the boiling broth and simmer, covered, for 20 minutes without stirring. Then stir once again to fluff up rice before serving.

Serves 8.

Arroz Especial

Special Rice with Carrots and Olives

> 2 cups white rice
> 1 green onion, minced
> ⅓ cup oil
> 4 tablespoons finely minced carrots
> ½ can ripe olives, or ½ cup
>   mushrooms, minced
> 4 cups chicken broth

Pour boiling water over rice in a bowl. Let stand for 20 minutes. Rinse with cold water, changing water 4 times until rice is free of starch. Simmer the onion in hot oil until wilted, then add rice and stir until every grain is coated with oil. Add carrots and ripe olives or mushrooms. Pour boiling broth over the rice and cover. Steam for 20 minutes until rice is tender. Stir to fluff it up and cover to keep warm until serving time.

Serves 8.

Arroz a la Mexicana

Mexican Rice

> *Boiling water*
> 2 *cups rice*
> 2 *medium-sized tomatoes, peeled and seeded*
> ½ *medium-sized onion*
> 1 *clove garlic*
> ½ *cup butter, or* ⅓ *cup cooking oil*
> *Salt*
> 2 *cups chicken broth*
> 2 *cups water*
> *Garnish with peas, avocado slices, stuffed green olives*

Pour boiling water over rice to cover and let rest for 15 minutes, then drain off water. Rinse 2 or 3 times under cold water to remove starch. Drain well and set aside. In a blender or food processor or by using a molcajete, puree the tomatoes and blend with the onion and garlic.

Heat oil in a heavy skillet and stir in the rice.

Fry rice until pale-gold over a high heat, stirring constantly. Add the puree and continue to fry and stir until rice is dry. Salt lightly and pour broth and water over the mixture. Lower heat to simmer. Cover and cook for 20 minutes until broth is absorbed. Then stir in hot, cooked peas and serve garnished with avocado slices or sliced pimiento-stuffed olives.

Serves 8.

Arroz Verde

Green Rice

>   2 *cups white rice*
>   1 *cup chopped parsley*
>   *Leaves from ½ bunch watercress*
>   ½ *cup chopped green onions*
>   1 *serrano chile, stemmed and*
>   *chopped*
>   1 *clove garlic*
>   ⅓ *cup oil*
>   1 *teaspoon salt*
>   4 *cups chicken broth*

Put rice in a bowl and cover with boiling water. Let stand for 15 minutes. Then drain and rinse with cold water until the rice is free of starch. Drain well and set aside. In blender or food processor, puree parsley, watercress, onions, chile, and garlic. Heat oil in a heavy skillet and add rice, stirring to coat it with oil. Add puree and continue to stir until the mixture is quite dry. Mix salt with broth and pour over rice. Stir once, then lower heat to simmer. Cover and steam for 20 minutes without stirring until water is absorbed and rice is tender.

Serves 8.

Arroz con Almejas

Rice with Clams

A dish that came to Mexico with the Basques.

> 2 *dozen clams in the shell*
> 3 *shallots, chopped*
> ¼ *cup olive oil*
> 2 *cloves garlic, minced*
> 1 *teaspoon paprika*
> 2 *tablespoons minced parsley*
> 5 *cups clam broth*
> 2 *cups rice*
> *Salt and pepper to taste*

Leave the clams whole in their shells; scrub well with a vegetable brush. Allow them to cleanse themselves by sprinkling corn meal over them and soaking them in water, in the refrigerator, for several hours or overnight.

Simmer shallots in oil. When transparent add garlic, paprika, and parsley.

Put the cleansed clams into a covered pot with a little water and cook over a low flame until the clams open. Reserve clams. Strain the juice through a double strainer. Add enough water to make 5 cups. Add shallot mixture, rice, salt, and pepper. Cover and simmer for 30 minutes.

Serve as a first course, or as an entree with a salad and fresh fruit.

Serves 6 as entree; serves 8–10 as first course.

Arroz con Jocoqui

Rice with Sour Cream

A sopa seca that makes an excellent accompaniment to broiled chicken or turkey.

> ½ pound Monterey Jack cheese
> 2 cups sour cream
> 2 cans green chiles, chopped
> 2–3 cups cooked rice
> Salt and pepper
> ½ cup grated cheddar cheese

Cut Monterey Jack cheese into strips. Mix sour cream and chiles together. Season rice with salt and pepper to taste, and in a buttered casserole layer the rice, sour cream and chile mixture, and the cheese strips. Make 3 layers until you finish with rice on the top. Bake at 350° for about 25 minutes.

Before serving, sprinkle cheddar cheese over top and allow to melt.

Remove from oven and serve.

Makes 6 servings.

Vegetables and Side Dishes

Mexican Corn Bread Soufflé

1 cup creamed corn (canned or
frozen will do)
2 eggs, beaten
⅓ cup corn oil
¾ cup milk
1 cup cornmeal
½ teaspoon salt
½ teaspoon baking soda
1 (4-oz.) can green chiles, diced
1½ cups grated sharp cheddar cheese

Preheat oven to 375°.

Combine corn, eggs, oil, and milk. Mix cornmeal, salt, and soda, and add dry ingredients to wet ingredients. Blend well with either a wire whisk or mixer. Pour half the batter into a lightly greased 1-quart casserole dish. Spread the chiles on top and sprinkle with half the cheese. Pour remaining batter over and sprinkle with remaining cheese.

Bake for 40–45 minutes.

Serves 6.

Minguiches de Jocoqui

Spinach-Filled Pancakes

Mexico's answer to the Italian cannelloni.

The Pancakes:
>1½ cups sifted flour
>1 teaspoon salt
>1½ cups milk
>3 large eggs
>Butter for frying

Mix the flour, salt, milk, and eggs, to make a thin pancake batter. Fry 1 at a time in a 6-inch frying pan, using 2 tablespoons of butter to start. Add more butter as needed to keep pancakes from sticking. Make 6 pancakes and set them on wax paper on a bread board or cookie sheet, and fill. Continue process until all batter is used.

The Filling:
>1 medium-sized onion, chopped
>1 tablespoon butter
>2 cups cooked spinach, chopped,
> drained, and seasoned
>½ cup cooked, minced ham or
> chicken or both

The Topping:
>2 cups sour cream or crema
> (see p. 210)
>½ pound Monterey Jack cheese,
> broken into bits

Sauté onion in butter until translucent. Add the spinach and ham or chicken. Place a spoonful of filling on each pancake, roll, and place seam side down on a buttered baking dish. Pour the sour cream or seasoned crema over the top and sprinkle with the cheese bits. Bake at 350° for 30 minutes.

If you are not a sour cream lover, make a white sauce with sweet cream, butter, and 4 tablespoons of flour and flavor with sherry.

Serves 6.

Nopales

Cactus Leaves

You may be able to live without nopales, the pulpy leaves of the cactus. But if you live near a border town you'll find them in the markets or in cans or jars, diced. They have a gentle flavor like some pallid squash. But most Mexican restaurants and family tables feature them regularly. They are best sautéed with onions and tomatoes; scrambled with eggs and chiles; or served with a vinaigrette.

Espinaca con Hongos

Spinach with Mushrooms

> 4 *bunches spinach, or 2 packages*
> *frozen spinach, chopped*
> ½ *pound mushrooms washed*
> ½ *medium-sized onion, minced*
> ¼ *cup butter*
> *Sherry or Madeira wine*

Wash and rinse spinach well and cook for 3 minutes only with the water that clings to the leaves. Chop or whirl in the processor until finely minced. If using frozen spinach, cook according to directions and drain well. Slice mushrooms and sauté in butter until barely cooked. Add the onion and cook for several minutes more. Then add the spinach and simmer until all vegetables are tender.

Just before serving add a dash of Madeira or sherry and heat for 3 minutes again.

Serves 6–8.

Ejotes con Jitomate y Chile

String Beans with Tomato and Chile

> 2 *pounds string beans*
> 1 *small onion, finely chopped*
> 1 *clove garlic, minced*
> 2 *small tomatoes, cubed*
> ¼ *cup butter or oil*
> ½ *cup canned chile sauce*
> 1 *teaspoon oregano*

String the beans and cut them diagonally. Cook uncovered for 15 minutes in salted water to cover. Drain thoroughly. Simmer onion, garlic, and tomatoes in butter or oil. When tomatoes are soft, add beans and chile sauce and cook for 10 minutes, covered. Rub oregano between your fingers and sprinkle over the cooked vegetables. Cover and let steam for a few minutes until ready to serve.

Serves 8.

Garbanzos y Jitomate

Garbanzos (Chick-Peas) in Tomato Sauce

> 1 pound garbanzos, soaked overnight
> 1½ quarts water
> 2 cloves garlic
> 1 medium-sized onion, chopped
> ⅓ cup olive oil
> 3 medium-sized tomatoes, peeled, seeded, and chopped
> 1 can pimientos, or 1 sweet red or green pepper, cut in strips

Drain garbanzos that have been soaked overnight. Add the water, garlic, onion, and olive oil. Cook for 1 hour, then add the tomatoes and continue cooking until the garbanzos are tender. During the last 10 minutes of cooking add the pimientos. If using fresh peppers, add them with the tomatoes.

Serves 6.

Calabacitas en Crema

Zucchini in Cream Sauce

1 *pound small zucchinis*
2 *medium-sized tomatoes, peeled,*
  seeded, and coarsely chopped
½ *cup heavy cream*
3 *sprigs fresh coriander*
1 *sprig fresh mint, or ½ teaspoon*
  dried mint leaves
3 *cloves*
4 *peppercorns*
2 *small fresh serrano chiles, finely*
  chopped (seeded, if you wish them
  milder)
Freshly ground pepper
Salt

Clean and trim zucchini, and slice into rounds. Combine all ingredients (except for the salt) in an earthenware dish. Cover and bake for 30 minutes in a preheated 350° oven. Sprinkle salt on top and bake for 15 minutes longer.

Serves 6.

Colache

Mixed Vegetables with Corn

6 *medium-sized zucchinis*
4 *ears corn*
1 *small onion, chopped*
¼ *cup butter*

2 medium-sized tomatoes, cubed
1 bell pepper, chopped
Salt and pepper to taste

Clean and trim zucchini and cut into ½-inch pieces. Cut the kernels from the corn. Sauté the onion in butter until translucent. Add the vegetables and seasoning. Simmer, covered, for 15–20 minutes until vegetables are cooked through. Stir occasionally to keep from scorching.

Serves 6.

Pimientos Frescos Asados

Broiled Fresh Red Peppers

Colorful and delicious!

2 fresh red bell peppers
1 clove garlic
¼ cup wine vinegar
½ cup oil
Salt and pepper to taste

Place fresh red peppers under the broiler, turning on all sides until skin blisters. Place in a paper bag, close, and let steam for 15 minutes. Remove thin skin, which should peel easily. Take out seeds and cut peppers into strips.

In a small bowl, mince garlic. Add vinegar, oil, salt, and pepper. Put peppers in the marinade and let stand for about 2 hours, unrefrigerated.

As an accompaniment to meat, serves 6.

CHAPTER X

GGGGGGGGGGGGGGGGGGGGGGGGGGGGGG

Egg Dishes

GGGGGGGGGGGGGGGGGGGGGGGGGGGGGG

The recipes that follow can be served at any meal, but are particularly good brunch fare. Served with fresh fruit and one of the wonderful Mexican drinks you'll find in the last chapter, any of these dishes can be the center of a festive brunch, made as easily as you can say "Egg McMuffin."

Huevos Rancheros

Ranch-Style Eggs

Traditionally, the eggs are fried, but I prefer them poached and served on lightly fried tortillas, topped with a piquant red or green sauce, and with frijoles refritos on the side.

> 2 *small tortillas, or 1 large tortilla*
> *(usually corn)*
> 2 *tablespoons butter or peanut oil*
> 2 *eggs*
> ½ *cup salsa ranchera (see p. 32) or*
> *salsa de chile pasilla (see p. 33) or*
> *salsa de tomatilla (see p. 36)*

Fry the tortillas lightly in oil and remove from pan before it gets crisp. Drain on paper towel and set in a warm oven to hold. Fry or poach the eggs, then place them on the tortillas (if using 2 tortillas, lay them on the plate so that one overlaps the other) and top with heated salsa (ranchera, chile pasilla, or tomatillo).

Serve immediately with frijoles refritos (see p. 159) on the side.

Makes 1 serving.

Huevos Rancheros para Fiesta

Ranch-Style Eggs for 12

> 1 *onion, sliced*
> 1 *clove garlic, mashed*
> 1 *green pepper, chopped*
> 3 *tablespoons butter or vegetable oil*
> 1 *tablespoon paprika*
> 6 *medium-sized tomatoes, peeled,*
>   *chopped, and seeded, or substitute*
>   1 *(28-oz.) can Italian tomatoes*
> 12 *eggs*
> *Salt to taste*
> 1 *teaspoon oregano*
> *Pinch cumin*
> *Chili powder to taste*

Sauté onion, garlic, and green pepper in cooking oil for several minutes. Add the paprika and stir well, then add tomatoes and cook for 10 minutes (less if using canned tomatoes). If possible, remove garlic and pour the sauce into a shallow earthenware or glass baking dish.

With a tablespoon, make a well in the sauce and slip each egg deep into sauce. Sprinkle lightly with salt and seasonings. (You may wish to grate cheese over the top as well.)

Bake in a 350° oven for 20 minutes.

Serve with warm tortillas, frijoles refritos (see p. 159), and arroz a la Mexicana (see p. 163).

Serves 12.

Chiles Rellenos

Chiles Stuffed with Cheese

> 1 (7-oz.) can green chiles, or 6 fresh
> California chiles
> ½ pound Monterey Jack (or cheddar
> or Muenster) cheese, cut in strips
> 3 eggs, separated
> ½ cup flour
> Salt and pepper to taste
> Oil for frying

If you are using fresh green chiles, roast them directly over a gas flame until the skin blisters. If you do not have gas burners, place the chiles under a broiler, turning to blister all sides. After blistering skin, wrap each chile in a wet paper towel and let cool, then remove skins.

Slit chiles enough to remove seeds and membranes, but try to retain the stem. If you are using the canned chiles, they will need just a little deseeding, but you will not have a stem.

Inside each slit chile, place a strip of cheese.

Beat egg whites until stiff. In a separate bowl, beat egg yolks until frothy. Add flour, salt, and pepper to yolks to form a thin batter. Then fold egg yolk into egg white.

Roll stuffed chiles in egg batter and fry in hot oil until brown. Drain well on paper towels and serve with salsa ranchera (see p. 32).

You can make the chiles rellenos in advance and reheat them in the salsa in a Pyrex dish or earthenware casserole. They will be delicious, but not as high and puffy as when they are first made.

Makes 6 chiles rellenos.

Chiles Rellenos Casserole

A California version of this famous Mexican specialty. Tasty and without oil, this makes an excellent brunch dish.

> 10 California green chiles, fire-roasted,
>   peeled, and seeded, or 2 (7-oz.) cans
>   green chiles, whole
> 1 pound cheddar cheese (or ½ pound
>   cheddar and ½ pound Monterey
>   Jack), cut into 3" × 1" strips
> 4 tablespoons flour
> 4 tablespoons half and half
> 4 eggs, lightly beaten
> Salt and pepper to taste
> ¼ pound cheddar or Monterey Jack,
>   grated
> Pepitas to garnish (you can use
>   sunflower seeds)

If using fresh chiles, roast and peel (see Chapter I), slit open, and remove seeds and stems. If using canned, slit open and remove whatever seeds and veins remain on chiles. Stuff each chile with a piece of cheese. Arrange chiles in a buttered casserole dish in either 1 or 2 layers.

In a mixing bowl, combine flour, half and half, and eggs. Beat slightly with whisk or fork until mixed (batter will appear slightly lumpy). Season with salt and pepper and pour over chiles. Bake in preheated 400° oven for 30–40 minutes.

Five minutes before serving, sprinkle top with about ½ cup grated cheese and a sprinkling of pepitas.

Wonderful served with fresh fruit and hot bolillos.

Serves 6–8.

Tortilla con Huevos

Tortilla with Eggs

> 1 *tortilla*
> 3 *tablespoons oil*
> 2 *eggs*
> *Salt to taste*

Tear the tortilla into bite-sized pieces and fry in oil until barely crisp. Beat the eggs, adding salt, and pour over fried tortilla, turning as you would for an omelette.

Even better if you sprinkle with fried chorizo.

Makes 1 serving.

Espárrago con Huevo y Queso

Asparagus with Egg and Cheese

> 1 *pound asparagus*
> ¼ *cup oil*
> 1 *clove garlic, peeled but left whole*
> 1 *small onion, minced*
> Pinch *oregano*
> 3 *eggs*
> 3 *tablespoons grated cheese*
> Pinch *nutmeg*
> Salt *and pepper to taste*

Wash and cut asparagus into 1-inch pieces. Heat oil in pan, add garlic, onion, oregano, and asparagus. Cover and cook slowly until asparagus is tender (about 12 minutes). Remove garlic.

Whisk eggs with grated cheese. When well mixed, pour over asparagus, stirring until eggs are set. Add a pinch of nutmeg, salt and pepper to taste, and serve.

Serves 4.

Chilequiles Oingo Boingo*

Tortilla Hash Oingo Boingo

> 4 tortillas
> Cooking oil or butter
> 1 green onion, minced
> ½ bell pepper, finely chopped
> 1 small tomato, peeled, seeded, and
>   chopped
> 4 eggs
> 4 ounces Monterey Jack or cheddar
>   cheese, broken into bits

Tear tortillas into small bite-sized pieces. Fry them in 2 tablespoons of oil until almost crisp. Still stirring, add onion and bell pepper and more oil or butter as needed. Add the tomato and cook, covered, for 10 minutes, until tomato is soft and mashable.

Beat eggs with a fork and pour over the mixture, and scramble lightly. Add cheese and cover, simmering until the cheese melts.

Serves 2.

Tortilla Española

Spanish Omelette with Potatoes

If you order a tortilla in Spain, you will be served an omelette, usually made with only eggs, potatoes, and

* A favorite of Sam Phipps, known to the music world as "Sluggo" and to Hélène as her son!

onions. In Mexico, the tortilla Española can be made with chopped green peppers, jalapeños, and even chicken or bits of ham. I like to bake the potatoes and scoop them from the shells, and then add them to the onions and butter.

 4 baking potatoes
 4 tablespoons olive oil
 ½ cup finely chopped onion
 ½ cup finely chopped bell pepper
 2 jalapeño chiles, seeded and minced
 1 teaspoon salt
 ½ teaspoon oregano
 8 eggs, beaten

Bake the potatoes for 1 hour, then scoop out filling from the shell. Heat the oil in a heavy skillet and sauté the onion, bell pepper, and chiles until wilted. Add the potatoes and mash them with a fork. Stir in salt and oregano, and pour in beaten eggs. Cover and cook over a medium heat without stirring for 10 minutes. If egg is not completely firm, pull the edge away from the pan and let any uncooked egg flow to the outside. When omelette is nearly set, place it under a broiler to brown lightly. Cut into wedges and serve with salsa fresca.

Serves 6.

▉▉▉▉▉▉▉▉▉▉▉▉▉▉▉▉▉▉▉▉▉▉▉▉▉▉▉▉▉▉

CHAPTER XI

Salads

▉▉▉▉▉▉▉▉▉▉▉▉▉▉▉▉▉▉▉▉▉▉▉▉▉▉▉▉▉▉

Tourists to Mexico are warned about eating any vegetables or fruit that cannot be peeled. The *ensalada* (salad) in Mexico usually consists of an ample serving of guacamole in a nest of lettuce. But in our country Mexican meals deserve the compliment of a salad and respond well to the additions of oranges or grapefruit, avocado, papaya, and jicama in various combinations.

Ensalada de Naranjas y Watercress

Watercress and Orange Salad

3 *bunches watercress*
8 *oranges, peeled and sliced*
3 *tablespoons olive oil*
Juice ½ lemon
1 *teaspoon dried tarragon*
Salt to taste
2 *green onions, finely sliced, or*
  ½ Bermuda onion, sliced

Remove most of the watercress stems, then make a bed of the leaves and place the sliced oranges over the base of greens. Mix oil, juice, tarragon, and salt, and pour over salad just before serving. Sprinkle with chopped onions or sliced Bermuda onion.

Serves 8.

Ensalada de Aguacate y Toronja

Avocado and Grapefruit Salad

Unless you are serving guacamole beforehand, this combination makes a delicious accompaniment to a comida Mexicana.

> 2 *heads Boston or butter lettuce, or*
>   *1 head of iceberg or romaine lettuce,*
>   *shredded*
> 3 *large grapefruit, or 3 cups canned*
>   *grapefruit segments*
> 3 *ripe avocados*
> 1 *sweet purple onion, thinly sliced*
>   *(optional)*
> ¼ *cup lemon juice*
> ½ *cup olive or salad oil*
>   *Salt and pepper to taste*

Line a flat dish or shallow bowl with Boston or butter lettuce leaves or shredded lettuce. Drain canned grapefruit and remove segments. If using fresh grapefruit, peel and separate segments, remove membrane. Peel and slice the avocados in half-moon shapes. Alternate avocado slices with grapefruit segments. Cover scantily with thinly sliced onion. Just before serving, pour over the marinade of lemon juice, oil, and seasoning. (Don't slice the avocados until ready to serve or they will darken.)

Serves 8.

Ensalada de Camarón y Chícharos

Salad of Shrimp and Green Peas

> 1 *head romaine lettuce*
> 1 *head iceberg lettuce*
> 3 *tablespoons white wine vinegar*
> 6 *tablespoons olive oil*
> ¼ *teaspoon tarragon*
> *Salt and pepper to taste*
> 2 *cups tiny Iceland shrimp or canned shrimp*
> 1 *cup shelled fresh or frozen peas, briefly cooked*

Tear—don't cut—lettuce into bits. Let shrimps and peas soak in the dressing until ready to serve. If refrigerated, remove from refrigerator 30 minutes before serving.

Pour shrimps and peas in their dressing over the lettuce and mix well.

Serves 8.

Ensalada de Noche Buena

Christmas Eve Salad

This is a festive and very traditional salad that is served in Mexico the night before Christmas. It is a favorite with everyone who enjoys a fruit salad with a few extras.

> 2 beets, cooked and sliced*
> 1 cup pineapple cubes, fresh or
>   canned
> 2 tart apples, peeled, cored, and sliced
> 2 oranges, peeled and sectioned
> 1 banana, sliced
> 1 lemon
> ¼ cup raw peanuts
> Seeds of 1 pomegranate
> 1 cup mayonnaise, thinned with
>   lemon or pineapple juice

In a large glass bowl, arrange all fruit and squeeze the juice of 1 lemon over all to keep from darkening. Sprinkle peanuts and pomegranate seeds on top. Add dressing or serve alongside in a separate dish.

Serves 6.

* Canned beets are acceptable, but fresh beets are preferable. Try cooking them in the oven, the French way. Simply wrap unpeeled beets in foil and roast in a slow oven for about 2 hours. Peel, slice, and use. The flavor is delicious.

Ensalada de Arroz

Rice Salad

This is a wonderful accompaniment to a spicy Mexican main dish and a pretty way to use up leftover rice.

> ¾ cup olive oil
> ½ cup orange juice
> ½ cup wine vinegar
> ¾ teaspoon salt
> 1 tablespoon grated onion
> 2 tablespoons minced parsley
> 3 tablespoons chopped pimiento
> 2 oranges, sectioned and seeded
> 2 packages frozen artichoke hearts, cooked and drained
> 5 cups cooked rice, cooled
> Tomato wedges
> Capers

Combine oil, orange juice, vinegar, salt, and spices, including pimiento and parsley. Blend together and let sit for about 30 minutes. Add oranges and artichoke hearts. Toss together with the cooked rice until blended. Refrigerate. Arrange on a platter before serving and decorate with tomato wedges and capers.

Serves 10–12.

Ensalada de Garbanzos y Pimiento

Garbanzo Bean (Chick-Pea) and
Pimiento Salad

1 (14-oz.) *can garbanzo beans, drained*
2 *tablespoons olive oil*
2 *tablespoons wine vinegar*
1 *tablespoon chopped parsley*
2 *green onions, minced*
1 *small jar pimientos or ½ fresh red*
   pepper, chopped

Rinse garbanzos in cold water. Combine all other ingredients, pour over garbanzos, and allow to stand for several hours before serving.

Variation: Mix red kidney beans and garbanzos in equal amounts.

Variation: Add kidney beans, wax beans, and green beans to garbanzo beans. Adjust amount of dressing and you have an excellent mixed-bean salad.

Serve instead of a vegetable with carne asada (see p. 123) or any chicken dish.

Serves 4.

Ensalada de Garbanzo

Garbanzo Bean (Chick-Pea) Salad

> 1 (14-oz.) *can garbanzo beans, drained*
>   *and rinsed*
> 3 *tablespoons lemon juice*
> 1 *tablespoon wine vinegar*
> ¼ *cup olive oil*
> 1 *tablespoon minced green onions*
> 1 *tablespoon minced parsley*
> 2 *tablespoons chopped bell pepper*
> ¼ *teaspoon dried oregano*
> 2 *medium-sized tomatoes, sliced*
> 1 *head Boston or butter lettuce*
> *Fresh basil (optional)*

Combine all ingredients except the lettuce and tomatoes and let marinate for about 2 hours. To serve, place several slices of tomato on a single lettuce leaf on each individual salad plate. Then add the garbanzo marinade. If you have fresh basil, place a few leaves on top.

Serves 4–6.

Pico de Gallo

Jicama and Orange Salad

> 1 *jicama, finely sliced*
> 2 *oranges, sliced then cut in halves*
> ¼ *cup chili powder*
> *Wedges of 2 lemons or 3 limes*

On a flat dish place the circles of jicama and on top of each circle half of an orange slice. Sprinkle lightly with chili powder. Place lime or lemon wedges around the outer edge of the plate.

Serves 6.

Ensalada de Arroz con Ejotes

Rice Salad with Green Beans

Another rice salad that can also serve as a vegetable dish.

> 3 *cups cooked rice, chilled*
> 1 *cup cooked green beans*
> ½ *cup chopped black olives*
> ¼ *cup diced pimientos*
> *Vinaigrette dressing (see p. 191)*
> *Salt and pepper to taste*
> *Tomato wedges*
> *Cilantro sprigs*

Combine first 5 ingredients. Season with salt and pepper to taste. Refrigerate overnight to blend flavors. Mix gently before serving. Garnish with tomato wedges and cilantro.

Serves 6–8.

Ensalada de Aguacate y Papaya

Avocado and Papaya Salad

> 1 *head romaine or butter lettuce*
> 1–2 *avocados*
> 1 *ripe papaya*
> ¼ *cup lime juice*
> ½ *cup olive oil*
> 1 *teaspoon salt*
> Pepper

Arrange lettuce leaves on 6 salad plates. Peel and slice avocados and papaya, and place alternate slices of each fruit on the lettuce. Combine the remaining ingredients and pour over all.

Serves 6.

Ensalada Mixta

Salad of Steamed Vegetables

This mixed salad is frequently seen on menus in Mexico and has a particular appeal for tourists who fear Mexico's raw vegetables.

> ½ *pound green beans, lightly steamed*
> 2 *cups cauliflower flowerets, lightly steamed*
> 2 *new potatoes, cooked*
> 2 *medium-sized carrots, lightly steamed*
> 1 *medium-sized zucchini, steamed*

1 small cucumber, peeled
1 bunch scallions
3 tablespoons chopped cilantro
Vinaigrette dressing
Salt and pepper
Lime wedges

Chop all vegetables in ½-inch cubes. Add cilantro and
toss lightly with vinaigrette dressing and seasonings to
taste. Chill well and serve with wedges of lime.

Vinaigrette Dressing:
⅔ cup olive oil
½ cup wine vinegar
2 cloves garlic, mashed
½ teaspoon each: tarragon, oregano,
Dijon-style mustard, and salt
1 egg
Sugar (optional)

Put oil, vinegar, garlic, herbs, mustard, and salt in blender
or a jar with a lid. Drop in the egg and blend or shake
until well mixed. A pinch of sugar can be added if desired.

Serves 6–8.

Ensalada de Coliflor Poblana

Cauliflower Salad from Puebla

> 2 cups thinly sliced cauliflower
> ⅓ cup finely chopped green pepper
> ¼ cup chopped sweet red pepper, or
>   1 (2-oz.) jar pimientos, sliced
> ½ purple onion, sliced
> Vinaigrette dressing (see p. 191)
> Salt to taste
> 1 ripe avocado, peeled and sliced
> Lettuce leaves

Combine cauliflower, green pepper, red pepper, and onion and mix lightly with oil and vinegar dressing. Add salt to taste. Refrigerate for several hours. When ready to serve, add avocado and toss gently. Spoon into a nest made of lettuce leaves. Add more dressing if needed.

Serves 6.

Ensalada de Totopos

Salad with Tortilla Chips

I have sneaked in the following recipe for Mexican taco salad, which is definitely more Southern Californian than Mexican. You can easily use the packaged tortilla chips, for it truly makes no difference in the final product. I have served it for luncheons with a batch of hot corn bread or the corn bread soufflé (recipe on page 167), to rave reviews.

1 head iceberg lettuce
1 red onion, thinly sliced
4 medium-sized tomatoes
2 ripe avocados, sliced
Vinaigrette dressing (see p. 191 or a
    good bottled dressing will do)
1 small bag tortilla chips
½ pound cheddar cheese, grated
1 pound lean hamburger
1 (12-oz.) can kidney beans
Salt and pepper

Combine lettuce, torn into bite-size pieces, and onions. Add tomatoes, cut into wedges, and avocados, and mix with about 1½ cups salad dressing. Make a small hole in the bag of tortilla chips to let out the air, and crush the chips inside the bag. Add crushed chips and grated cheese to the dressed greens, but do not toss.

Brown hamburger and drain off all liquid. Add the kidney beans (drained) to the meat and warm. Season to taste. Put warm meat mixture on top of salad and mix briskly. Serve immediately.

Serves 6.

Note: For a lighter variation of this salad, substitute chicken for hamburger, and Monterey Jack for cheddar.

CHAPTER XII

Desserts

Polvorones

Cinnamon Tea Cakes

>   1 cup butter
>   ½ cup powdered sugar
>   2¼ cups sifted all-purpose flour
>   ½ teaspoon cinnamon
>   ¼ teaspoon salt
>   1 teaspoon vanilla
>   2 cups powdered sugar and
>   1 teaspoon cinnamon for rolling

Cream butter and add sugar, flour, cinnamon, salt, and vanilla to make a moderately stiff dough. Chill in refrigerator for a few hours or overnight, then roll into small balls about 1 inch in diameter. Bake on a buttered cookie sheet in a 400° oven for 14–17 minutes. While still warm roll the tea cakes in the sugar and cinnamon mixture. Cool on a wire rack, then roll in sugar and cinnamon again.

Makes about 4 dozen.

Buñuelos

Tile-Shaped Fritters

Fiesta cookies really, the size of large tortillas. They can be enjoyed whole or broken into pieces and served in bowls with a thin brown sugar or maple syrup.

> 4 *cups sifted all-purpose flour*
> 2 *tablespoons sugar*
> 1 *teaspoon baking powder*
> 2 *teaspoons salt*
> ¼ *cup melted butter*
> 2 *eggs, beaten*
> ¾ *cup milk*

Sift dry ingredients into a bowl. Beat the eggs and milk together and add to the dry ingredients. Add butter and mix into a dough that can be easily handled. A bit more milk may be added if the dough is too sticky. Turn it out onto a lightly floured board and knead until smooth.

Divide the dough into 20 pieces and shape into balls. Cover with a cloth and let stand for 20 minutes. Roll each ball into a round about the size of a large tortilla, or into a square shape the size of a large tile. Let stand for about 5 minutes, then deep-fry in hot oil until light golden-brown. As each one turns crisp, remove it to drain on paper towels. They may be sprinkled with cinnamon and sugar or served in a bowl with syrup. Wrapped tightly in foil they freeze well. To crisp, loosen foil and heat in a 300° oven before serving.

Makes about 2 dozen large buñuelos.

Torta de Almendras

Almond Torte

A Mexican dessert of Spanish descent that is very popular in the elegant private homes of Mexico City. The top is decorated with blanched almonds arranged like daisy petals with chocolate bits for the center, making a beautiful dessert.

> 9 eggs, separated
> Pinch salt
> Peel of 1 lemon, grated
> 1½ cups sugar
> ½ pound unblanched almonds

Beat egg whites with pinch salt until they peak but are not too dry. Whisk together the egg yolks, lemon, and sugar. Grate the almonds in a blender and add to the egg yolk mixture. Fold together egg whites and yolk mixture.

Pour into a well-buttered spring-form pan and bake in a preheated 400° oven for 30 minutes.

Churros

Mexican Crullers

A Mexican cousin to the American doughnut or the French cruller, the churro is wonderful served with coffee or chocolate on a chilly morning. Children find them wonderful any time of the day, in any weather!

>1 cup sifted flour
>1 teaspoon salt
>1 cup boiling water
>1 egg
>Oil for deep frying
>1 slice bread
>½ lemon, wedged
>Powdered sugar

Sift flour and salt into a mixing bowl. Make a well in the center of the flour and pour in boiling water. Beat with a whisk until fluffy and smooth. Add the egg and continue to beat until the batter is smooth and shiny.

Fill a deep pot with enough oil to deep-fry. When the oil is heated add a slice of bread and the lemon to the oil. Leave in until the bread turns very dark, then remove bread and lemon. They will give the churros a distinct taste.

Pour batter into a pastry tube and squeeze small cylinders (3–4 inches) into the hot oil. When churros are golden-brown, remove and drain on paper towels. While still hot, roll in powdered sugar.

Makes 12.

Flan Sencilla

Plain Caramel Custard

The classic Mexican dessert that you'll find on every menu, served in every home.

> ¾ cup granulated sugar
> 3¾ cups simmering milk (richer and
>   creamier if made with half and half)
>   1 stick cinnamon
>   2 teaspoons pure vanilla
> Pinch salt
>   5 eggs
>   4 egg yolks

Bring ½ cup granulated sugar to the boiling point, stirring continually until caramelized to a deep-amber. Remove from heat and continue stirring until all lumps dissolve. Then pour quickly into a 6- to 8-cup mold and turn it in all directions to coat the sides. When caramel ceases to run, turn mold upside down until ready to be filled.

Heat the milk, add ¼ cup sugar, cinnamon stick, and vanilla. Salt and let simmer for 10 minutes. Meanwhile, beat eggs and egg yolks together. Stir them into the hot milk mixture. Strain through a sieve into the caramel-coated mold. Set in a pan of boiling water (baño de María—Mary's bath) and bake for 50 minutes. To test if done, insert a silver knife—the blade should come out clean. Refrigerate.

Remove from refrigerator and bring to room temperature before unmolding.

Serves 8–10.

Flan de Calabaza

Pumpkin Flan

From Helen Brown's Holiday Cookbook comes this very different flan that is perfect for Halloween or Thanksgiving, both pumpkin pie occasions.

1⅔ cups sugar
3 cups half and half
2 cups drained, canned pumpkin
1 teaspoon salt
¼ cup Jamaica rum
6 eggs

Put a cup of sugar in a small saucepan over low heat and allow to melt, stirring constantly until it turns a deep-amber. Quickly remove from heat and pour into a round deep dish that will be used to bake the custard. Tip quickly in all directions so that the sides of the dish will be coated with caramel.

Meanwhile, scald the cream. Add pumpkin, salt, the remaining ⅔ cup of sugar, rum, and lightly beaten eggs. Pour the mixture into the dish and place in a pan of water (Mary's bath). Bake at 350° for 1 hour or longer, so that a knife inserted into the center comes out clean. To keep a crust from forming, you may cover the dish with a layer of foil.

When cool, invert on a round serving dish. Serve chilled or warm, with a dollop of whipped cream; or flame it with rum.

Serves 6–8.

Flan de Fiesta

Festive Flan

1¾ *cups sugar*
3 *egg whites*
8 *egg yolks*
Pinch *salt*
2¾ *cans condensed milk*
¼ *cup strong coffee*
2 *teaspoons vanilla extract*
4 *tablespoons dark rum*

Put 1 cup of sugar into a heavy pan and place it over a low flame, stirring constantly until it turns a deep golden-brown. Remove instantly and pour into mold in which the flan will be baked. Tip the mold around until all sides are coated with caramel. Let cool while making the custard.

Beat whites and yolks together with a fork or wire whisk until light and lemon-colored. Add remaining sugar, salt, milk, coffee, vanilla, and rum. Strain into the coated mold. Cover with foil and place in a pan of boiling water that reaches more than halfway up the outside of the mold. Bake in a 350° oven for 1 hour or more. Test for doneness by inserting a broom straw or a silver knife. If it comes out clean, refrigerate flan until serving time. Bring to room temperature and unmold.

When ready to serve, pour heated brandy over it and bring it to the table flaming.

Serves 6–8.

Note: If serving to a crowd, double or triple the recipe and bake the flan in a large earthenware cazuela or casserole. Don't bother to unmold—just pour the heated brandy over the top and flame it gloriously.

Brazo de Gitano

Gypsy's Arm—Cake Roll with Cream Filling

5 eggs, separated
⅔ cup sugar
⅛ teaspoon salt
1 tablespoon water
1 cup cake flour
Cinnamon and powdered sugar for
    dusting

Beat egg yolks, sugar, salt, and water until thick and creamy. Add the flour and beat just enough to blend. Fold in stiffly beaten egg whites. Spread evenly in a 10-by-15-inch cookie sheet lined with heavy paper. Bake 10–15 minutes in preheated 375° oven until cake is lightly browned on top and springs back when touched with a finger. Turn it upside down on a sheet of waxed paper sprinkled with powdered sugar and cinnamon. Cool; then trim the brown or ragged edges. Spread with filling and roll. Remove the wax paper, and keep in refrigerator until serving time. Sprinkle with cinnamon and powdered sugar.

Rum Custard Filling:
2¾ cups milk
1 vanilla bean cut in pieces, or 1
    teaspoon pure vanilla
¼ cup dark rum
½ cup sugar
3 tablespoons cornstarch
3 egg yolks
2 tablespoons sweet butter

Cook milk, vanilla bean, and rum over low heat. Allow to boil slowly for 5 minutes. Beat sugar, cornstarch, and egg yolks until thick and creamy. When milk is cool, strain it into the egg mixture, beating constantly. Cook, stirring over low flame until thickened (about 20 minutes—do not let it boil). Just before taking from fire, add butter and stir until blended. Cool before filling the cake.

Serves 8–10.

Biscocho con Crema Caramela

Sponge Cake with Cream Caramel Filling

The Cake:

>   7 *eggs, separated*
>   1 *tablespoon lemon juice*
>   1 *cup sugar*
>   ¼ *teaspoon salt*
>   1 *tablespoon dark rum*
>   1⅓ *cups flour*
>
> *Caramelized custard filling*
> *Powdered sugar for dusting*

Beat yolks with lemon juice until light-yellow. Add sugar and salt and beat until stiff. Add rum and flour and beat just enough to mix. Whisk egg whites to stiff peaks. Add 3 drops lemon juice as eggs begin to whiten. Fold into cake dough and spread evenly in 2 pans, buttered and sprinkled with flour. Bake 15 minutes in a 425° oven, until cake is lightly browned and springs back when touched with a finger. Invert pans. Don't remove cakes until they cool.

Caramelized Custard Filling:

> 3 cups milk
> Peel of 1 lemon
> 2 sticks cinnamon
> 4 egg yolks
> 1 cup sugar
> 3 tablespoons cornstarch
> 1¼ tablespoons butter

Bring milk to a boil with lemon peel and cinnamon sticks broken into small pieces. Boil slowly for 5 minutes. Beat egg yolks with ½ cup sugar and 3 tablespoons cornstarch until light in color and stiff. When milk is cool, strain it into the egg yolk mixture. Blend and stir frequently while cooking over low heat until mixture thickens (about 20 minutes). Do not boil. Just before removing from fire add butter and stir until melted and blended. When cool spread thickly over 1 layer of the cake. Sprinkle with the remaining sugar, then place the layer with the custard under the broiler until sugar browns and bubbles. When sugar is caramelized, place top layer over the filling. Sprinkle powdered sugar over top of cake. Refrigerate.

Serves 8–10.

Suspiros

Chocolate Meringues

Suspiros are wonderful little chocolate kisses, with just a hint of cinnamon. They are an attractive accompaniment to fresh fruit, following a grand Mexican meal, and can be stored in your kitchen in an air-tight jar and kept fresh for a week.

4 egg whites, room temperature
¼ teaspoon cream of tartar
¼ teaspoon salt
1 teaspoon vanilla
1 cup sugar
2 ounces Mexican chocolate, or 2
   ounces semisweet chocolate, grated,
   flavored with 1 teaspoon ground
   cinnamon

Heat oven to 350°.

In a deep bowl—copper is best—beat egg whites until foamy. Add cream of tartar and salt and continue beating until egg whites form stiff peaks. Beat in vanilla and sugar until the meringue is stiff and shiny. Fold in the grated chocolate.

Using a large tablespoon, drop individual dollops of meringue on an ungreased cookie sheet. Place in oven and immediately turn off the heat. Let the meringues sit in the oven for 3 hours, without opening the oven door.

Remove baking sheet from oven and tap the bottom lightly to loosen the meringues. Cool on a cake rack and store in an airtight jar.

Makes about 4 dozen.

Empanadas de Dulce

Sweet Turnovers

Empanaditas filled with meat or cheese or shrimps are fine with cocktails. But by adding sugar to the dough and filling the little crescent-shaped turnovers with applesauce or jam or French custard cream, you will have a nice tea cake or dessert.

2 cups all-purpose flour
2 teaspoons baking powder
2 tablespoons sugar
1 teaspoon salt
½ cup shortening
⅓ cup ice water
Applesauce, jalapeño jelly, raspberry
    jam, or French custard cream
1 cup sugar
1 tablespoon cinnamon

Sift flour, baking powder, sugar, and salt into a bowl. Work the shortening in as you would for pastry. Add ice water sparingly, just enough to hold dough together. Divide dough in 12 even-sized pieces. Roll each one out on floured board to make a round about 4 inches in diameter. Place a spoonful of applesauce flavored with cinnamon, jalapeño jelly, raspberry jam, or French custard cream on half of the rounds. Fold the other half of the pastry over the filled half, pressing the edges firmly to seal in the filling (dampened fingertips make it easier). Bake in a 400° oven for 15–20 minutes. While still hot, dip them in a mixture of 1 cup sugar and 1 tablespoon cinnamon.

Makes 12 empanadas.

Cajeta de Membrillo

Quince Paste

Served with creamy Teleme or Monterey Jack cheese, or even with a simple cream cheese, quince paste is delicious either as a dessert or as an afternoon accompaniment to tea or wine. Guava and mango pastes are equally pleasing and are made in essentially the same manner.

1 *pound quince*
1 *pound sugar*

Wash quince and steam until tender, about 20 minutes. When cool enough to handle, cut in quarters and remove seeds and cores. Grind through the finest blade of a food chopper (include the skins), measure, and place in a deep saucepan. Add an equal amount of sugar and begin to stir over a medium flame.

The mixture will thicken as you cook. Stir continuously until it is quite thick—thick enough to see the bottom of the pan. Pour the mixture into a square or oblong loaf pan that is lined with wax paper. Set it aside for about 24 hours. (Traditionally, it is placed on a waxed paper–covered board, covered again with cheesecloth, and placed in the sun for 2 days, turning the *cuero* from time to time to make sure all sides are exposed to the sun.)

When it is set—either in your kitchen or out in the sun—remove from the dish and wrap securely in tin foil. It will keep in the refrigerator for weeks.

Helado de Mango

Mango Ice Cream

Mangoes in Mexico are very tempting when you see them being sold in the marketplace or on the street corners, strung like great golden beads on five-foot poles. But they are safer to eat at home, fresh or canned. With a good processor, mango ice cream is the simplest of desserts— even simpler if you have an electric ice-cream freezer.

2–3 *cups whipping cream*
1 *cup light cream*

½ cup sugar (*if the mangoes are fresh and green, additional sugar will be needed*)

3 mangoes, peeled and cut in chunks

Heat the cream and sugar and bring just to a boil. Skim and add to the mangoes in the blender or processor jar. Process for 5 seconds, then turn into a mold and freeze. Process and refreeze twice before serving. If you are using an electric ice-cream maker, follow the directions given.

Serves 4–6.

Sorbete de Papaya

Papaya Sherbet

2 *ripe papayas*
½ *cup orange juice*
1 *tablespoon Grand Marnier or other liqueur*
½ *cup sugar*
½ *teaspoon fresh lemon juice*

Remove seeds and skins from papayas and dice fruit. Combine all ingredients in a food processor or mixing bowl and beat well until smooth.

Pour into a refrigerator tray or shallow pan and freeze until sherbet is mushy. Remove from freezer and stir vigorously. Refreeze until mushy again, and repeat stirring. Return to freezer until ready to serve.

Serves 6.

Mangos Diablo

Flambéed Mangoes

> 1 tablespoon butter
> 1 tablespoon sugar
> 1 lime or orange
> 2 ounces Triple Sec
> 3 mangoes (or peaches), peeled and
>   sliced
> 2 ounces tequila

Melt the butter in the pan of a chafing dish. When very hot, add sugar and stir until dissolved. Pare the lime or orange and add the parings to the chafing dish. Add the Triple Sec and flame it in the pan. When the flame dies down, remove lime or orange peel and add the juice. Stir until mixture is reduced and begins to thicken.

Add the fruit and, as the syrup begins to bubble, add the tequila and flame again.

Serve over French vanilla ice cream or sponge cake. Garnish with whipped cream.

Serves 6.

Salsa de Frutta

Fresh Fruit Sauce

Served as an accompaniment to fresh fruit, such as melon, papaya, mangoes, pineapple, or berries.

> ¼ cup sugar
> ¼ teaspoon freshly grated lemon rind
> ¼ teaspoon freshly grated orange rind
> ⅓ cup fresh orange juice
> ¼ cup fresh lemon juice
> 2 egg yolks, beaten*
> 2 cups heavy cream, whipped

In the top of a double boiler, combine and heat sugar, lemon and orange rinds, and juices. When hot, pour a few tablespoons into the beaten egg yolks, beating quickly to prevent the yolks from cooking. Then slowly beat egg mixture into fruit mixture and continue stirring over simmering water until mixture is thick enough to coat a spoon.

Cool to room temperature. Fold mixture carefully into whipped cream. Mix well and chill. Serve with fresh fruit or berries.

Makes approximately 2½ cups.

* Use your egg whites to make suspiros, see page 203.

Higos con Crema

Fresh Figs with Cream

Historically sinfully sensual, this fig dish is a visual delight as well. Especially if you have grenadine on hand to give the crema a little color.

>2 figs per person
>Crema (see below)
>Few drops grenadine

Slice fresh figs crosswise and use only the largest circles. Each fig should yield about 3 good round slices. For each guest, use a shallow dish—glass or pottery—or even a shallow soup bowl. If you wish the crema to take on a pink tinge, add a few drops of grenadine, stir briskly, then cover the bottom of the serving dish with ½ inch crema. Arrange the figs in eye-pleasing configurations. When figs are in season, this is a simple and delightful finale to a Mexican comida.

Crema

Mexican Sour Cream

Close to *crème fraîche* in taste, lighter than commercial sour cream, crema goes as well with enchiladas as it does with fruit. Simply add 3 tablespoons of buttermilk to ½ pint of whipping cream. Let stand in a warm place for 6 hours. Stir occasionally. Place in refrigerator overnight to thicken.

CHAPTER XIII

Drinks

Mixed Drinks

Non-Alcoholic Drinks

About Mexican Beer

Mixed Drinks

Alcoholic drinks (copitas) in Mexico are created for one end result—passion! Even those drinks without the fire of aguardiente, tequila, mezcal, and rum—the non-alcoholic drinks of tamarindo, Jamaica (flower of the hibiscus), and orchata (made with rice powder)—are soothing and sensual. Even Mexican chocolate, tea, and coffee tease the senses with the unexpected hint of cinnamon.

Tequila

This potent drink made from the magnificent maguey plant, in its pristine form is served in a small slender glass on a ceramic saucer with a slice of lemon and a mound of coarse salt. Dip the lemon in salt, savor its bite, then sip the tequila.

In the cantina, a jigger of tequila—glass and all—is placed at the bottom of a stein and a bottle of Mexico's wonderful beer is poured over it . . . a boilermaker with a Mexican accent.

The Margarita

> 1 *part tequila*
> 1 *part curacao or Cointreau*
> *Juice of ½ lime*

Pour ingredients over crushed ice and stir, or blend vigorously with cracked ice until slushy. Rub the rim of a glass with lime then spin it in coarse salt. Strain the liquors into the cocktail glass and sip through the rim of salt. If you prefer a frothier drink, add a slight spoonful of egg white before blending.

Makes 1 drink.

Sangríta–or Sangre de Viuda

Widow's Blood

One sip of sangríta to quell the fires of the slender cylinder of straight tequila. Serve ice-cold tequila in one glass, the sangríta in another. Trade sips.

> 3 ounces tomato juice
> 1 teaspoon or less of grenadine syrup
> Juice ½ lemon or 1 lime
> ¼ ounce orange juice
> Salt
> Chopped ice
> 1½ ounces tequila
> Chopped serrano chiles, cilantro

Shake all ingredients with chopped ice before adding the tequila. If you don't have serrano chiles add Tabasco sauce to taste.

Makes 1 drink.

Tequila Bloody Mary

> 6 ounces tomato juice
> 1½ ounces tequila
> Dash Tabasco sauce
> Several squeezes lemon
> Few drops Worcestershire sauce
> Cilantro, parsley, oregano, or basil leaf,
>   finely chopped
> Lemon or lime wedge

Mix the first 5 ingredients and pour over ice. Sprinkle any or all of the herbs on top. Serve with a wedge of lemon or lime.

Makes 1 drink.

Mezcal

A curiosity for Anglos, especially the bottle with the ornate label and the worm of the maguey visibly floating inside. The round black ceramic bottles from Oaxaca are collectors' items, as are the black ceramic monkeys with bright bibs and aprons. Despite the worm, which shows the mezcal is authentic, this liquor is a bit smokier than tequila and a bit smoother to the taste. It is especially delicious when served with a float of apricot nectar over ice.

Toro Valiente

Brave Bull

> 2 *parts tequila*
> 1 *part Kahlúa*
> *Cracked ice*
> *Lemon peel twist*

Stir tequila and Kahlúa over cracked ice. Strain into a cocktail glass and add a twist of lemon peel.

Makes 1 drink.

Vallarta Fizz

2 *jiggers tequila*
1 *teaspoon sugar*
1 *egg white*
Cracked ice
1 *lime*
Dash grenadine
Club soda

Blend tequila, sugar, and egg white vigorously with cracked ice. Add the juice of the lime and a dash of grenadine and blend again quickly. Strain into a tall 8-ounce glass and fill with cold soda water.

Makes 1 drink.

Piña Colada

3 *ounces coconut milk*
3 *ounces pineapple juice*
3 *ounces light rum*
Crushed ice
1 *slice pineapple*

Put all ingredients except the pineapple slice in the blender. Blend until frothy and pour into a chilled glass. Garnish with the pineapple.

Makes 1 drink.

Coco Loco

This can be delicious or a disaster, depending on how many ingredients are left in and how many are left out.

> 1 large fresh coconut
> 1½ ounces light tequila
> 1 ounce light rum
> 1 ounce Myers's rum
> 3 ounces pineapple juice
> 3½ ounces coconut milk
> 6 ounces crushed ice
> ½ ounce Kahlúa (optional)
> ½ ounce 151-proof rum, or 1 ounce
>   Spanish brandy
> 2 lime wedges

With an ice pick and hammer, poke a hole in the eye of the coconut. Drain and reserve the milk. Then cut off the top of the coconut with a Chinese cleaver, just as you would cut the top off a Halloween pumpkin.

In the blender, mix tequila, light and dark rum, pineapple juice, coconut milk, and crushed ice, and Kahlúa, if desired, until frothy, and pour into coconut shell. Float the 151-proof rum or brandy. Garnish with lime wedges. Serve with straws.

A loving cup for 2 people.

Note: If fresh coconut is not available, you can substitute powdered coconut and increase pineapple juice to 6 ounces. To serve this version, a large brandy snifter or bowl-shaped glass can be used.

Sangría Roja

Red Sangría

> 4 *oranges*
> 2 *lemons*
> 2 *peaches*
> 1 *apple*
> 1 *pear*
> ½ *cup sugar*
> ½ *cup brandy*
> 1 *quart red table wine*
> *Champagne or charged water*

Slice oranges, lemons, and whatever other fruit is in season. Place them in a punch bowl or sangría pitcher and cover with ½ cup sugar and ½ cup brandy. Soak for several hours or overnight. Before serving add a large chunk or mold of ice and a quart of red table wine. Add as much champagne as you wish, or just enough charged water to give the sangría a bit of zest.

Variation: 1 pint orange juice, 1 quart burgundy, 2 ounces curacao, charged water, and ice.

Makes 10–12 drinks.

Tequila Daisy

> 2 *jiggers tequila*
> ½ *jigger lemon juice*
> ½ *jigger grenadine or maraschino juice*
> 1 *jigger club soda*

Mix ingredients. Shake vigorously with ice and strain into a cocktail glass.

Makes 1 drink.

Tequila Sunrise

2 teaspoons grenadine
Crushed ice
2 ounces white tequila
4 ounces orange juice
Club soda

Pour the grenadine over crushed ice in a tall chilled glass. Mix the tequila and orange juice and pour over the grenadine. Fill the glass with club soda, but stir very gently, so that it resembles a sunrise.

Makes 1 drink.

Coctel de Presidente

Rum Martini

1½ ounces white rum
¼ ounce dry vermouth
1 slice lime

Mix rum and vermouth in a tumbler filled with ice. Serve with a twist of lime.

Makes 1 drink.

Sangría Blanca
White Sangría

    3 *oranges, finely sliced*
    4 *lemons, finely sliced*
    1 *cup sugar*
    1 *apple or pear*
  ½ *cup tequila, kirsch, brandy, or vodka*
    1 *bottle white wine*
    1 *bottle champagne or club soda*

Place the oranges and lemons in a crystal punch bowl or pitcher. Sprinkle with sugar. Add finely sliced white flesh of apple or pear. Pour ½ cup of liquor over all and mix gently. Let soak overnight or for several hours before serving. Add a large chunk of ice (I freeze mine in a coffee can) just before serving. Pour in a large bottle of white wine—and, at the last minute, add champagne or, more conservatively, club soda.

Makes 10–12 drinks.

Rompope
Eggnog

Serve as a liqueur, cold, or poured over fruit and ice cream. When bottled and corked tightly, it can be kept refrigerated for months.

    1 *quart milk*
 1¼ *cups sugar*
     Vanilla bean
  10 *egg yolks, well beaten*
 1½ *cups white rum*

Combine milk, sugar, and vanilla bean in a saucepan and bring to a boil. Reduce heat and simmer, covered, for 20 minutes. Cool to room temperature, then remove the vanilla bean and whisk the egg yolks slowly into the milk mixture. Add rum, decant into bottles, and cork tightly. Keep refrigerated at least 48 hours before serving.

Makes 12 small servings.

Kahlúa Egg Cream

No eggs in this one. Just Kahlúa and cream and a dash of club soda over lots of ice.

Café Libre
Iced Coffee with Rum

Fill a tall glass with cracked ice, add a jigger of Myers's rum, and fill to the top with strong coffee. Add sugar, whipped cream, or ice cream depending on your mood and the time of day.

Café Diablo
Coffee with Orange-Flavored Brandy

To a cup of strong coffee, add slice of orange rind, lightly scorched, then add brandy and sugar to taste. Top with whipped cream. A dessert in itself!

Non-Alcoholic Drinks

Agua de Flor de Jamaica

On a hot day in the plaza or the marketplace, vendors with gigantic jars of sweetened lime, orange, or watermelon water not only attract the eye but can quench your thirst. The flor de Jamaica (hibiscus) petals give a beautiful reddish-purple tinge to the iced water and is used by the Jamaicans in their rum punches. Flor de Jamaica can be found packaged in many local supermarkets along with tamarind. Follow the instructions on the package or try the recipe below that uses less sugar than would be acceptable to the Mexican palate.

⅔ cup dried flor de Jamaica petals
1½ cups cold water
½ cup granulated sugar
Water to make 4 cups of liquid

Put the dried flowers and 1½ cups water in a saucepan and boil for about 3 minutes over a quick flame. Add sugar and the rest of the water and leave in a glass container overnight. Strain the liquid into a glass pitcher and serve well chilled.

Makes 10–12 drinks.

Orchata

Described by adults as liquid rice pudding and adored by young aficionados, this drink is made of powdered rice, condensed milk, and cinnamon and tastes very much like Thai tea. It can be found packaged in Mexican mercados in the West and Southwest and perhaps, now, even in New York. Follow the instructions on the package or try to make your own with the ingredients mentioned above.

Fruit Drinks from the Blender

In every marketplace and bus station in Mexico, the blenders at the sheltered counters whir away, creating all kinds of drinks with the fresh fruit that always seem to be in season. Nothing is better on a hot day than these drinks. Our favorite is the strawberry.

> 1 *cup fresh strawberries*
> 2 *tablespoons powdered sugar*
> 1 *cup cold milk*
> *Shaved ice*

Blend all ingredients and serve in a tall frosty glass.

For a change, substitute pineapple, papaya, apricot, banana, or peach, adjusting sugar to sweetness of the fruit.

Melons, too, take on a new dimension when blended with milk and sugar. If you use watermelon, blend with ice (no need to add milk or sugar) until the liquid is a lovely pale pink, then serve over ice.

Chocolate

The chocolate drinks in Mexico are special because Mexican chocolate circles contain cinnamon as well as chocolate and sugar. The circles divide easily into quarters. Use ¼ of a circle for each cup of milk. When the milk is heated and the chocolate dissolves, put the pretty wooden *molinillo* into service and whisk the liquid into a creamy foam. If you can't find the yellow-and-red-striped cylinder with Ibarra's signature, add a touch of cinnamon to your favorite chocolate mix.

Tea

A stick of cinnamon in the water you boil for tea will give the drink a Mexican flavor.

Café de Olla

In a glass or earthenware pot bring water to a boil; add 3 tablespoons of coffee (coarsely ground) and a 1-inch stick of cinnamon. Add dark-brown sugar to taste and bring to a boil twice. Strain and serve.

About Mexican Beer

Few people realize that Mexico is one of the world's major brewing nations, and not too many beer drinkers realize that Mexico brews beers that closely resemble the great German pilsners and bocks. Again we have Maximilian to thank for introducing the Viennese brewing traditions to a country that had been brewing beer since 1594. In Mexico, cerveza (beer) has a higher alcoholic content than is allowed for export to the United States and therefore is quite different from the Mexican beer you will find here. So while in Mexico enjoy a chilled stein of draught beer in Monterey or a bottle of Carta Blanca or Bohemia. In Tecate, try the beer that is brewed close to the border in Baja California. In Veracruz you'll enjoy Dos XX's, the mellow dark beer or the lighter Tres XXX. And at Christmastime watch for the rich, dark Noche Buena that occasionally appears in local markets here.

Index